A
Nervous Challenge

Rob Platts

Published by Monnaie Publishing
Copyright © Rob Platts

Cover picture courtesy of Mark Windsor. All other pictures courtesy
of Mark Windsor and Mark Dravers

All profits from the sale of this book will go
to the MS Society's Guernsey Branch

Ros once said: 'You love that boat more than you love me!'
'No,' I said, 'I love you both the same.'

We're still laughing.

This book is dedicated to:

The rowers

Ian Atkinson
Robbie Beck
Andy Chapple
Trevor Coulter
Colin Fallaize, MBE
Geoff Gavey
Matt Harradine
Adie de Kooker
Sam de Kooker

John Lewis
Joe Paul
Lloyd Le Page
Karl Pederson
Stephen Pipe
Colin Robert
Mark Shepherd

The support team

Colin Cherry
Geoff Cullington
Joan Cullington
Tony Cullington
Jane Cullington
Mark Dravers
David Farrimond
Dr Ian Gee
Dave Hadlington
Liz Hendry
Ron Hendry
Jason Hobbs
Karl Van Katwyk

Geoff Van Katwyk
John Van Katwyk
Roger Martell
John Neale
David Read
Stuart Rowe
Garry Seabrook
John Tostevin
Jon Travers
Mark Vaudin
Buz White, MBE
Mark Windsor

and to all our sponsors for their generous support.

Contents

Preamble

In writing the first draft of "A Nervous Challenge", I did so simply to record the extraordinary effort so many Guernsey folk put into one sporting event in support of a charity. Originally I wanted to record the detail because I was concerned that, like my Grandfather who also had Multiple Sclerosis (MS), at some point, my memory loss and cognition impairment might become severe. Of all the things I have been involved with in my life, the London to Paris Row, even though I personally did not row a single stroke, is one of the projects of which I am most proud.

The event was staged to raise money to employ a much-needed specialist nurse, who would provide essential therapies and help to the 150 islanders in Guernsey who have MS, and to provide support for the families of people who have the disease. I may be wrong but I believe the row raised more money than any single sporting charitable event had ever raised before in Guernsey.

Mark Windsor, who is a friend, journalist, writer and photographer, read the first draft and suggested I should include some more detail about my life and my motivations – I found this process excruciatingly difficult. However, I also discovered that this examination of my own experiences had a surprising effect.

Like most people, I enjoy receiving praise; within my story of MS I talk about the vain and pathetic wish that people would recognise that I was facing MS with strength.

These self-centred thoughts confused me. It took me a while to realise just how vain these were, and that actually I am my own harshest critic.

When I finished the first draft of this "memoir" back in 2004, I concluded that what really mattered was that I should be able to be happy with myself, that I should do all that I can to make living with MS easier for my wife, and that I should try to be a good model for my children. If you manage to read this story through to the end you'll see that even these seemingly simple life goals have changed somewhat as a result of further curve balls that life has thrown at my family.

There is always a danger, of course, of going too far with this human interest stuff and slipping into self-absorbed rubbish, which I find can be unattractive and difficult to read. So, I hope I have the balance right, and, that by following Mark's suggestion, I might have brought a bit more depth and interest to the account of the row and to my experience of living with MS and, at the same time, spread some greater awareness of the disease in general.

Everyone's experience of living with MS is different, but I suspect the fear, the sense of loss, and the harrowing feeling of being lost in uncertainty, comes at some point to all who receive a diagnosis of MS.

For the most part I have had a charmed, comfortable and privileged life and, for at least half of the years since my diagnosis (1991 to present, 2014), the disease has been in remission. I have been relatively fortunate with the course of the disease in that I have experienced almost no restriction in my mobility; not so fortunate, but then again, not disastrous either, in how it has affected me, so far, in other ways.

If you are reading this account as someone who has been recently diagnosed, you will probably already appreciate that there is no way of predicting the physical, mental and social effects of the disease. However, if you gain nothing else from reading this, I hope you may gain some confidence, and confirmation, that the human mind can cope with some extraordinary challenges and that human beings are capable of the most remarkable acts of kindness and charity in order to bring comfort and solace to others.

Chapter One – Beginnings

"You're not to go chasing fishes
'til you've done those dirty dishes,"
my mother used to say.

Not listening to her wishes,
I did go chasing fishes,
figuring, in my simple way,
that those boring dirty dishes,
unlike cunning little fishes,
aren't too likely to swim away

***

Arthur Ransome has much to answer for, as far as my life experiences are concerned. My generation is amongst the first to have been lucky enough to be inspired, and magically transported, in adventure and imagination, by his books. His most famous work, Swallows and Amazons, quite literally changed my life. That book sparked a lifetime of fascination with the sea and boats and perhaps, if I had never read it, I might not have ended up living in the wonderful island of Guernsey, and the following account might have been very different, or might not have happened at all.

My father was a doctor in the British Army and, in the '50s, he was stationed in Austria, where my brother was born, and then in Germany, where I made my debut appearance. When my Guernsey friends first discovered my country of birth, I was subject to a prolonged and generous helping of light-hearted mockery, as, during the Second World War, soldiers from Germany were, shall we say, "visitors without invitation" who imposed their will on what has always been a fiercely independent little nation.

1

Beginnings

Dad was raised in a loving, but somewhat Victorian atmosphere, and I think his strict mother, his formal schooling, followed by the discipline required by medical school and the army, together instilled in him a moral code and sense of duty, discipline and social expectation which might seem almost antiquated now. He was probably born after his time. His is a difficult example to follow. I am acutely aware of the social advantage my father's hard work brought to me and my siblings, and, while I believe I share his sense of social duty, his attributes of orderliness do not come naturally to me.

I'm not sure why, but I've always disliked schedules, routines, and repetitive events.

My Nan, my mother's mother, always prepared fish on Friday, for instance; not through any religious reason, and to me, this was anathema. Yes, I loved her homemade battered fish and twice-cooked chips, but if all Fridays are predictable, then, to my mind, they are unlikely to be exciting, adventurous and new. I suppose some may see this as an attitude of a privileged life, where, maybe I have been sheltered from the need of the comfort and the certainty which can be found in routine. It has always been my view that this certainty is mostly illusionary and that, the only certainty in life, apart from the clichéd "death and taxes" is that nothing, absolutely nothing, is certain. The irony of the uncertainty of MS, though, is not lost on me. Perhaps by generally inviting uncertainty into my life this has, in a strange way, helped me live with the disease.

My parents moved back to England when I was still a baby and Dad joined a small medical practice in Watford, Hertfordshire. Home was always full of the wonderful smells of my mother's cooking and the sound her opera singing.

My older brother, David, was an extraverted, energetic and demanding child, who was always a bit rebellious and

2

often in mischievous trouble. Being the first-born son, however, meant that he carried my father's expectations and aspirations in a heavier way than I ever had to.

David and I fought constantly, as some brothers do, but I think my mother was totally unprepared for the difficulty which can result from when two sons are so different and don't get along. Mum was a gentle and graceful woman and not really cut out for disciplining us and adjudicating our disagreements.

The wonderful cooking smells, and the beautiful sound of my mother's singing, were sometimes tempered therefore, not just by our sibling squabbles but also by Mum getting upset at her inability to deal with us. I think our household invented the saying, "wait 'til your father gets home." Perhaps, if we could have appreciated how petty and insignificant our childish arguments were, in comparison with the difficulties she faced as an evacuee during the Second World War, being sent, at the age of nine, 4,000 miles away from home to live with strangers, and being responsible for looking after her little brother, then maybe my brother and I might not have tested her so.

Unhelpfully perhaps, Dad wasn't much good at discipline either. I suspect he was incredibly well behaved as a child and that dealing with two warring boys wasn't in his skill set either.

His military background might have led him to believe that a loud voice and the threat of more severe discipline would bring results, but he surely didn't see that the results mostly came through fear, rather than through achieving a genuine wish within us to improve our behaviour. He didn't mean to be, but his military approach and some of the terms he used, were, however, amusing. When we were teenagers, and he was intent on getting us up and ready for school, he would stand on the landing and boom such things as "Right you horrible lot! -

Beginnings

Hands of cocks, on with socks – your turn in the bathroom, Robert - you lazy swine".

I have two younger sisters, both of whom were born in England. When my sister Elizabeth was born I think both parents were relieved the new baby wasn't another boy. Thereafter, the dynamics of the family changed somewhat. Elizabeth was a daddy's girl from day one. I soon discovered that my title of "youngest child" had been usurped by the horrible title of "middle child". As such, in terms of expectations, aspirations and even care needs, I was something of a child without portfolio.

However, being quieter than my brother, and perhaps more self-sufficient than either of my siblings, meant that this changed order oddly suited me. My new place in the family meant that, by and large, I was left to play happily in Rob's make-believe world of adventure; but it did leave me feeling rather disconnected from the rest of the family.

Mum and Dad didn't produce Alison, my youngest sister, until I was nine, and such was the age gap that her arrival was no threat to the established hierarchy and I think she was able to enjoy being universally welcomed by her older siblings, but she, too, probably has her own take on this.

I was about 7 or 8 when I started to become fascinated by the world around me. I started to collect all manner of objects, not to make collections, but rather to see how they worked, or to make use of them. These things included mechanical items as well as creatures of all sorts, alive and dead. Old wind-up gramophones, clocks, watches, and even ancient electric toasters found their way in to my bedroom to be dismantled, without necessarily ever being reassembled.

I fancied myself as a bit of an inventor too, but my attempts at using a wind-up clock mechanism to automatically open and close my bedroom curtains, for instance, never really came to much.

Beginnings

A bit like Gerald Durrell, I too was fascinated by wildlife and I was forever bringing home stray dogs, birds with broken wings, hedgehogs full of fleas, sticklebacks and leeches from the local river, and numerous and various road kill, for dissection, or consumption (if they didn't smell too bad). In fact, a succession of wildlife, dead and alive that tested my mother's patience.

I had a pigeon living in my bedroom for quite a while – pigeon pooh everywhere. "Have you been letting that filthy pigeon loose in your room again Robert?" Mum used to scream. "Me? No! It just escaped," I would fib lamely. Mum always called me Robert when she was cross; Rob, or Robbie even, when I was in her good books, or when she wanted me to do something for her. I was a busy lad, always far too busy to waste time on chores, which included homework and washing up.

I shouldn't give the wrong impression about my self-sufficiency, though. Yes, I was happy with my own company but I was "a sensitive boy" as my mother described me. However, I reckon most teenagers go through stages of feeling that nobody understands them and then, that the world is a terrible place that needs their influence to put things right. Mum liked the fact that I was sensitive and was so proud when, at aged 11, I came second in a local poetry competition. For many years however, I did wonder if Dad felt this wasn't perhaps a sign of weakness. Not the coming second – the poetry writing. Dad's very upright character and sometimes stern demeanour didn't always allow him to show his true feelings towards David and me. Years later, and only after I had a steady girlfriend, my mother, showing some prejudice perhaps, admitted that, she thought I might be gay. Obviously, in my case, my teenage angst and paranoia were well placed.

Since my mother passed away in 2013, I have spent more time with my father and we have grown together

5

through our grieving. I've discovered that behind that sometimes brusque exterior, lies the tenderest of hearts. I think maybe in the past, I in turn may have misunderstood him.

***

I mentioned Arthur Ransome's books, but for those not fortunate enough to have read them, I should explain. His books with their completely absorbing tales of children adventuring on the Norfolk Broads, and even of finding themselves accidently at sea, made me seek out every opportunity to get on or in the water.

I was never a very good Christian, but I thought a few hours of being pumped full of religion was a fair trade to be able to join the canoeing club operated by the Crusaders (a Christian Youth Association) on Saturday afternoons. This was the first time I had been in a canoe on my own, and it was every bit as exciting as Arthur Ransome's books.

Drug therapy for my MS, and the MS itself, has caused me to have what I describe as a "Swiss cheese" memory. I have no control over what or when I remember things, but the memory of my first solo trip in a canoe is something I doubt, or at least sincerely hope, will never leave me. It is hard to describe the allure of boating; Ransome managed it wonderfully of course, but for me, boating is an escape, a guaranteed adventure, and very often a challenge which rewards perseverance and skill.

I had walked, played by, and fished the river Gade often, but that day, there was the excitement of adventuring on that little river which meant it took on a completely different character. Going gently with the current, you become part of this living thing.

The shallow, bright, lively, sparkling and quietly chattering and gurgling water was full of mystery and promise. The banks were brushed with the pastel colours of wild flowers and watercress, and brought alive by the movement of brightly decorated dragonflies and even the flash of the odd, darting kingfisher. The real magic though, was that I was in control, and I was voyaging somewhere. Always with boating, danger is a part of the excitement. The little river in Cassiobury Park, for that short time one Saturday afternoon in July, became the Amazon – I was facing, and conquering, fear and danger, and, in my mind, nobody had ever explored that wild river before.

Between the ages of about 5 and 12, we lived in a house quite close to the Grand Union Canal, and when I reached the age of 10, I was allowed to visit the canal without supervision. From then on, I spent every moment I could fishing it, swimming in it or trying to build something that floated on it.

I think when my father saw my attempts at raft building (the first was made with oil drums, strapped together with a pair of his old braces), it had him thinking about the possibility of the family owning a craft that might be a little safer, and less likely to fall apart.

Then, one day, my father came home with a brochure of a small dinghy - a sort of semi-catamaran design, called a "Romany Cat", which could be rowed, sailed, or powered by a small outboard engine. 'Platypus', as Dad decided to name her, was made of blue polypropylene and virtually indestructible. Platypus sealed the deal. I was officially obsessed with boats.

After prep school, I followed my brother and attended Watford Grammar School for boys. On my first day, such was my brother's reputation, that my teacher asked, 'Which one of you is Platts?' and instructed me to sit at the front of the class.

I wasn't much of a student. If I found a teacher inspiring I did well, but if the pace was slow or I didn't like the teacher, I just switched off and daydreamed. To illustrate this, there was a history teacher who brought the subject alive. He was enthralling, and under his influence I did well. Unfortunately he left the school, and he was succeeded, in my O-level year, by a dusty historian who possessed a voice which, if a drug company could bottle it, would have done away with the need for sleeping pills forever. Worse, he seemed to be going through the motions of teaching, whilst completely unaware of the students around him. I was quickly bored, and made little effort.

Towards the end of that year he said to me, 'Platts, there is little point in you attending my class: you have no interest in history and I have no interest in you. I suggest you spend the rest of your history lessons in the library, where you can continue your daydreams undisturbed.'

I failed history O-level with an unclassified mark. I am very much to blame, I accept that. But later, in business, I was always on the lookout for dreamers, because, they can be both your best asset and your greatest threat.

As our schooling progressed, it was obvious that brother David was never going to shine academically (although once in a work environment he became an unstoppable achiever) and, even though I was doing little better than he was, I felt the weight of dad's aspirations subtly shifting my way.

Dad was happy that I had an interest in science and, although I don't think he ever said it, there was definitely a feeling that he wanted one of us to follow in his footsteps and study medicine.

But I had no wish to be a doctor. In those days GPs worked crazy hours, night and day, and they were not particularly well paid. It seemed to me that Dad spent the best part of his working life trying to keep up with the societal pressures of being a doctor. Most people assumed that doctors were rich, or at least comfortably off. There was an expectation amongst my father's peer group that they would live in a detached house, they would have a car or possibly even two, and that their children would be educated at private schools.

Dad did actually managed to provide most of these things, but I believe at some cost to his physical and mental wellbeing. Mum was as guilty as anyone at succumbing to these social pressures and, although I'm sure she didn't intend to add to Dad's stress, her feeling a need to "keep up with the Joneses" certainly did have this effect.

My parents never said it, but I sensed, when I became comparatively wealthy at a young age and retired early, that there was some envy. I'm not suggesting for a minute that Mum resented my success, but I think she saw it as not quite fair that Dad had studied and worked so hard, held a position of significant responsibility, and saved and improved so many lives and yet was not as well materially rewarded as their caterer son.

My seeing how my father had struggled, did not make the prospect of becoming a doctor seem attractive. Thankfully, pay and conditions for doctors are generally much improved – a good job since both my daughters have chosen medicine as a career.

These improvements came too late for me though, and instead, I decided I wanted to be a marine biologist. When I was younger, I mistakenly thought Jacques Cousteau was a marine biologist (he was actually the co-inventor of the aqualung and a world renowned ocean explorer). Marine biology seemed to fit well with what, by now, was an all-consuming passion for all things to do with the sea and boats and my interest in science.

In my teens I also became interested in racing sailing dinghies. I know Watford may not seem an ideal part of the world for sailing, but a little gravel pit near Rickmansworth was good enough for me. Incredibly, even my earlier experience of canoeing paled when compared to being at the helm of a sailing boat. A canoe, unless a river current is taking it, requires the input of man's energy to propel it. A sailing boat has an endless source of energy. With a scrap of cloth and a small boat you can, quite literally, sail around the world.

But it was also the speed of sailing that excited, and still does excite me. It wasn't long before I was consumed by dinghy racing. I got into sailing to such an extent that I gave up rugby, much to the disgust of my rugby coach, who was always giving me stick about it, telling me I'd gone soft. That was, until I persuaded him to come out with me one day when the weather was particularly blowy and rough. He was white when we got back to shore and was good enough to acknowledge that sailing was not some sort of sissy option.

I learned to swim at a young age and I think I was the only boy in the first year of my prep school who could already swim. Whilst my fellow students were having swimming lessons in the shallow end of the school pool, I was allowed to pretty much do what I wanted. This usually involved pearl diving of course (picking up stones from the bottom of the deep end). All this ended, however, when the Head Master, Mr Sobers, who wasn't aware that I could swim, walked past the pool one day, saw me at the bottom, and jumped in, wearing his best tweeds, to save me.

Whilst at the Grammar School, I had yet another watery adventure that involved swimming pools and head masters.

I was keen to be able to prolong the sailing season. Normally we sailed right up to the end of October, but it had become so cold that sailing had become painful. In those days, we just sailed in whatever we had on, usually jeans and a sweaty waterproof top. There was none of this fantastic high-tech specialist go-faster, breathable sailing gear that kids can benefit from today.

When the weather was blowy and we needed more weight to keep the boat upright and sailing fast, we just put on a big jumper and jumped in the water before the race (against the rules now). We didn't have changing rooms or showers either, we used to cycle the six miles to the lake and the six miles home again, dripping wet.

This was bearable in the summer, but I think we were seriously in danger of hypothermia as autumnal weather arrived. So, to extend the season, I needed a wetsuit. A wetsuit would of course be essential too, if I was to become Jacques Cousteau the second. Anyway, Mum and Dad came to the rescue and gave me a wetsuit kit for Christmas. It consisted of a great role of neoprene and a huge pot of smelly glue.

By this time, we had moved from the house near the canal and now actually lived opposite Watford Grammar School. This was great in the sixth form, for nipping home to have a fag with my mates and great too, for illicit use of the school's open-air swimming pool.

Eventually, my Mum insisted that the school made the Platts' house out-of-bounds during break times as the pigeon pooh in my bedroom had by now been caked over with a generous brown layer of tar, deposited by the cheap and nasty cigarettes I, and most of the sixth form, smoked in those days.

Anyway, having put aside all school work and chores in order to concentrate on what really mattered, by the end of January, I had achieved my goal – I had finished the wetsuit.

Of course, now I needed to test the suit to make sure it worked and to make sure that I had glued all the seams properly.

It got pretty dark by 6.00 pm and, confident that the teachers would have gone home; I donned my new wetsuit and put a knee-length coat over the top. With mask and snorkels under my arm, I, and my now black neoprene legs, proceeded to walk across the road to the school. I was about halfway along the road to the pool when, to my horror, I spotted Trog (Mr Turner, the head teacher) walking straight towards me. I couldn't turn and run, so I just kept walking. As I approached, he greeted me with a smile and said, "Nice night for it," and that was it! I couldn't believe it, but he obviously hadn't realised what I was up to – either that or he had more of a spirit of adventure than a headmaster has a right to possess.

I ran over the school field and scaled the low fence (unthinkable now, but back then, that was all that guarded the pool). In the pitch dark, the water appeared to be inky black. It was very spooky and, for a second, I did wonder at the wisdom of swimming here, on my own, on a dark January night.

I leapt in and came up gasping with the shock of just how cold it was. I had no control over my breathing and my heart was beating at a ridiculous rate. Fortunately, the wetsuit worked, and, after the initial shock, the layer of water, trapped by the suit, started to get a bit warmer. Even so, I didn't manage more than a couple of minutes in the water which must have been near freezing. My heart took another leap when something solid brushed up against me as I swam.

That was it; I'd had enough and couldn't get out fast enough. I went back to the pool the next day with my school pals to look at the pool in daylight. It was a shame I hadn't thought to reconnoitre the pool earlier, as the water was green and the mystery object in the pool turned out to be a park bench that someone had thrown in. This was an early lesson in event planning and risk assessment.

Beginnings

***

I stood, waiting and looking through the glass
Until, when the light of day had gone,
(I don't recall the moment, precisely)
the window glass had become looking glass,
and I no longer saw love shining eternally.
I saw only my reflection, looking back, patiently.

***

After Grammar School I applied to Bangor University, which was reputed to have one of the best marine biology departments in the country. My interview with an old professor in his cluttered office was a surprise to me. Behind him on the wall, in an enormous glass case, was a large piece of seaweed. Almost as soon as I sat down, the professor asked "Well young man, are you able tell me what that is in that glass case?"

I couldn't believe it. I only knew the name of one seaweed and this was it. I knew the answer because this particular weed had been in the news recently, for being a possible threat to British harbours and marine life.

"Sargassum," I said.

"Good heavens," he replied, "You are the first student, in all my years, to ever get that question right."

The professor was obviously impressed, but I was still surprised that the university offered me a place, subject to my achieving three Cs at A-level, which was pretty generous. Useless student that I was, I didn't even manage that. However, my grades did allow me entry to an alternative course, and I scraped in to read biochemistry and soil science.

Beginnings

So, off to Bangor it was, and I was lucky enough to rent a cottage on the side of a mountain, about 20 miles away from the campus. The cottage had been in a friend's family for centuries and was in a breath-taking and isolated location on the side of a mountain, with views over fields lined with dry stone walls, to the Menai Straits and Anglesey.

My parents drove up to Wales with my belongings and, because my motorbike was quite slow, I went ahead the day before. Mum and Dad spent the night in the little spare room. Mum was frightened by the location and worried about leaving me there on my own. She sobbed as she said goodbye.

The cottage was quite basic and set up more as a summer holiday home. Heating was by one log fire and one small electric stove. The electricity for cooking and lighting was via a prepaid meter. The bathroom was in a sort of lean-to with a corrugated iron roof. Sometimes I ran a hot bath just to get warm but, it was so cold most of the time, that when I did, the whole cottage filled with steam.

I loved living in the cottage, but I was quite cut off from my fellow students – actually, pretty much isolated from civilisation altogether. I don't think I would have minded, but a few months before, I had met my first serious girlfriend, Sally, and was desperately lovesick.

Like most students, I'd never had to manage my own money before. I think I'm right that Bangor has more pubs in its high street that any other in the UK. My new friends and I visited most of them more often than we should have, and it wasn't long before my funds were running pitifully low. Added to the traditional student faux-pas of too much alcohol, during the first few weeks, I spent money I couldn't afford on two trips to London to visit my girlfriend.

Beginnings

The first part of the journey to London was beautiful, as it took me on sweeping, winding roads, around the base of Mount Snowden – fabulous on a motorbike in good weather. The rest of the journey was less appealing, as it entailed joining the A5, a Roman road, which was dead straight, almost all the way into the centre of London: dead straight but monotonous and freezing cold. The first time I did the trip back to London, the cold forced me to break the journey. I found I was shaking uncontrollably and starting to fall asleep. Fortunately a lovely lady in the roadside café took one look at me and sat me in the warm kitchen, next to an open oven door. The next time I attempted that journey I wore my trusted wetsuit under my wax cotton motorcycle gear. As it turned out, this was just as well. The weather had been foul, with heavy winds, rain and sleet and, as I was rounding Snowden again, I came across a river of water and mud flowing across the mountain road. As I tried to stop, I skidded, and the bike slid on its side, through the freezing water. Thankfully the bike and I were OK and, because of the wet suit, I was able to carry on to London. That night I re-united with my girlfriend in her brother's pub, the Royal Oak at Watford, and was met with howls of laughter from the regulars when I stripped off to my wetsuit.

I was so broke, I ended up living on whatever food I could catch or gather and I didn't have enough money to feed the electricity meter and heat the cottage properly. I didn't feel I could ask Dad for any more money, mostly because he would have been furious that I had spent it all on booze and trips to see my girlfriend. To survive, I ate porridge, and drank milk, which was delivered daily to my door. I fished, snared rabbits, picked blackberries and once even kept a sea bass in the bath for three days. But that was all I ate. I have never been so hungry. To my shame, I even conveniently put aside my father's lessons on moral fibre and fair play, in order to dodge the milkman for a week or two because I had no money to pay him. On one occasion I saw him coming up one side of the mountain and so I freewheeled on my motorbike down the other side, to avoid paying him.

It didn't take long for me to realise that the University course was of no interest to me. I was desperately unhappy. I was alone in this freezing cottage on the side of a mountain in Wales and I just wanted to be with my girlfriend, but I couldn't see a way out.

The village near to my cottage was mostly Welsh-speaking and was not at all welcoming to a student from England. I came back to the cottage from university one day to find "F***k off back to England" writ large in fresh paint on the garden gate. I used to lie awake at night, listening to the wind and to the sheep moving on the dry stone walls, wondering if it wasn't innocent sheep but instead some liberator of Welsh cottages come to burn me in my bed. The doorbell to the cottage was a miniature brass bell, like a ship's bell, and, when the wind was howling and caught it, this used to toll, mournfully, on its own. I slept with a bread knife and an old sickle under my bed.

Clearly this couldn't carry on, but I felt trapped. I was the only one of the four children to make it to university and I felt I would be letting my parents down if I didn't continue. My brother and I had disappointed Mum and Dad all through our school years, and me giving up university would just be the last straw. I suppose though, this was the point that I started to grow up.

I was beginning to realise that dreams were all well and good, but there was no point in trying to live somebody else's. I would have to square up to some hard facts and be truthful with my parents and, perhaps more importantly, with myself. So, I gave up university and returned to Watford. The truth is, and this was not to be the last time in my life, that love prevailed.

Beginnings

Having returned to Watford while I tried to work out what to do, I found a job working in a laboratory for a year. I also worked in a pub and really enjoyed the work. Finally, I settled on a new career and applied to go to catering college. I had three amazing years at Ealing Technical College, with a lot more food involved than during my short time at University. During my last year at catering college I won a scholarship to spend a few weeks studying contract catering in Canada. Slightly fatter, and much happier, I started work for a contract catering company, Sutcliffe Catering. Sutcliffe gave me time off for the Canadian trip and Sally came with me.

We both loved Canada and I was quite torn as, whilst there, I was offered a job, with a big salary, a car and a house. The only problem was that the job was way up in Northern Manitoba, in a place called The Pas. The Pas is quite isolated and miles from anywhere else and, of course, a long way from family or friends. Sally sobbed all the way on the flight back home and made me promise to take her back to Canada one day.

She and I decided to set up home together and we bought a little two-up / two-down in Brentford. But our relationship wasn't to last. Sal worked for the BBC and her life outside our relationship, working with talented programme makers and celebrities, became all-consuming. At first, she tried to involve me and I was often invited to watch the shows and join the after-show parties. But within a year of buying the house, she had met someone else and moved out.

For a while, I was devastated. I was struggling at work too. By now I was managing 13 catering contracts. Managing these contracts well required a massive commitment in terms of time and energy and, as well as being distracted by my failed relationship, it didn't help that I had a boss who I didn't rate and didn't much like. I made a couple of stupid mistakes and my boss hauled me in front of "the Admiral", our director of operations, who laid it on the line. Either I shaped up or he would fire me.

While, on this occasion, I hated his approach, I knew the Admiral was actually a decent chap. I suspect his approach may have been influenced by my immediate boss. I knew my future was in my own hands and I got things back on track. Within a couple of years my immediate boss was moved aside, partly through my ambition I suppose, and I was flying. At the age of 27 I was managing the largest and most profitable area within the company, with 70 contracts and a team of about 700 people.

Work-wise, things were going well, despite a few false starts, but I hadn't found my soul mate. It's said that sometimes you meet the right person when you are not looking and so it was that a little Welsh girl, full of fun and passion for life, walked into my life.

Ros was the manager of the team at a catering venue within Austin Reed in Regent Street, where we operated both the public restaurant and the staff dining room.

Right from the start I enjoyed her company, but I was Ros's boss and I was immediately torn between doing my professional duty and wanting to get to know her better. But, I'm only human, and increasingly I would find myself popping in to see her at Reed's restaurant.

Actually, at first I thought she wasn't interested in me because a few months before, because her visa had expired, she had been forced to leave her boyfriend, Kip, who lived in Kenya. Kip and Ros had been at college together and Ros followed Kip back to South Africa and lived with him there for a year.

Understandably, she was deeply affected by this enforced separation, but she says she had always felt that it would not last, and that while she loved him, she suspected that one day he might drift away. Some years later, after Kip had indeed found someone else, married and had children, Ros received the news that Kip and his stepdaughter had been tragically killed by a flash flood whilst providing support for a rallying event.

Ros says that she remembers the first time she saw me. She had gone to Sutcliffe's head office in Acton and she overheard me on the phone. She turned to look at me and maintains it was love at first sight, saying to herself, apparently, "That's the man I'm going to marry."

Ros and I started a secret relationship; it had to be discreet because office romances were frowned upon and I could have lost my job because of it. However, it quickly became serious. I was left wondering how and indeed whether, I could clear it with my boss.

I decided to come at the problem laterally. I decided to try and square it with our client at Austin Reed. I figured if Austin Reed didn't object, then it might be alright with Sutcliffe. I knew I was risking my job, but love won through. I could find another job but I wasn't going to lose Ros.

I was actually shaking with nerves when I went to see one of the senior management team at Reeds. I had arranged to meet with Tony Schooling, our client, and came straight out and told him I was having a relationship with Ros and was going to ask her to marry me. His reaction was totally unexpected. Laughing, he said: "If I wasn't already happily married I would have asked her out myself – good choice, Rob."

When I then approached the Admiral, I don't think he was delighted, but by then he had much more confidence in me and accepted the situation as a fait accompli.

Around this time I experienced what I now realise was probably an early sign of MS. I had a day were I was completely exhausted. But this was not normal exhaustion it was like I had been switched off, both bodily and mentally. It was as if I was wading through treacle. At the time I assumed I had a virus of some sort, but the symptoms were dramatic enough for me to remember this episode years later.

Ros and I married six months later at a beautiful chapel in Mayals, near Ros's home town of Swansea.

We honeymooned on a flotilla holiday in Turkey. It was a bit of a gamble on my part because Ros had never sailed in a yacht before, but fortunately she loved it and we have returned to Turkey almost every year since.

Ros had got interested in catering when she took a part time waitressing job whilst still at school. She then applied to Brighton Polytechnic (now University) to do an HND in catering management –the same course I did in Ealing. She is very different from me, though. She's quite a forceful character but sometimes endearingly unsure of herself. Neither of us is overly confident, I more than she perhaps. With Ros, if something is troubling her, we will all know soon enough. She is the glue that holds our family together, but at the same time, she can be a bit of a worrier. She'll take on the anxieties of our daughters, Katie and Sophie, and try to do the worrying for them.

A couple of years before I met Ros, I met another dreamer. You might recall my previous cautions about the power of dreamers, but Bill Baxter, my future business partner, was subtly different. But, I doubt he considers himself a dreamer. I'm not sure Bill ever did have a grand plan, more an unstoppable drive, sometimes consisting more of sheer likeability and charm than anything else. Bill was four years younger than me and when we first met he was working for Sutcliffe, but he was working in another area. I saw the potential in him and quickly manoeuvred him into my team.

I knew it wouldn't be long before he outgrew my team though, and it wasn't many years before people in the company were speculating that one day, he and I would possibly be vying for the top job in the company. I'm glad it never came to that.

Beginnings

During my last few years with Sutcliffe catering I became increasingly frustrated at the way the business was being run and I felt the company was placing short-term profit before long-term stability. I may have been running one of the largest teams within the company, and certainly one of the most profitable, but the resources available to assist me in terms of area management staff were inadequate. I often felt we could be doing a better job and that we could have been better employers.

It was about this time that I read a book about self-belief and motivation and I remember reading: "If you can't change from within, then get out and do it yourself."

I reckoned I had identified a gap, or at least a flaw, in the market and decided maybe it was time to do my own thing.

Bill and I shared a love of fishing and we socialised a lot outside of work. During our numerous fishing trips together we inevitably talked about the future. Bill still believed that he had a great future within Sutcliffe's, but even he was slightly unnerved by what was happening to some of the older managers in the business. One or two guys who'd given the company many years of service were sidelined or even let go when their face didn't seem to fit so well anymore.

We came to the conclusion that we would go into business together, but Bill and I didn't just automatically assume it should be contract catering. We considered a number of other alternatives including a tobacco vending business, a fish farm and even a toffee apple-making business.

But it didn't take us long to see the limitations of all these businesses and we settled firmly back on to the original idea of starting a rival business to Sutcliffe. Bill and I spent the next few months researching and writing a business plan. We reckoned we should be able to start our new company with £15,000 each which we could get from re-mortgaging both our houses. Further backup cash flow was secured through overdraft facility from Barclays Bank.

Now all we needed to do was push the button, resign from our jobs, and set about setting up Baxter & Platts Ltd.

The day before Bill and I were due to see the Managing Director and give notice, Bill called me. He said that he'd changed his mind and couldn't go through with it. He'd recently received a promise of further promotion and thought he'd be crazy to give up a big salary and nice car. I asked him to at least meet with me to talk it through, and we agreed to meet in the pub.

I had made up my mind that whatever Bill decided, I'd go ahead with the new business. I knew my chances of being successful on my own would be much reduced, but again, this was my dream, and I'd never forgive myself if I didn't give it a go.

Quite a few beers later, and only a short while before closing time, Bill changed his mind again and said he was now committed to us going in to business together.

I was worried that in the morning, when the beer had lost its effect, Bill might waver again; but he was now resolute, and Baxter & Platts was formed soon after.

A lot of water has gone under the bridge since those days and perhaps in the future I will set down on paper some of the details of the 10 exciting helter-skelter years of Baxter & Platts, but this is not the book in which to do that.

When I reached 40, we sold the business; Bill built up another business and sold that, and went on to become a major shareholder in yet another very large catering company.

Together, he and I had won every industry award going, including a "Catey" each, which is the hospitality equivalent of the film industry's Oscar.

Beginnings

A couple of years ago, Bill rang me: "Plattsy, you've got to keep this quiet, but I wanted you to be the first to know - I'm getting another award, can't flaming believe it, I'm being made a Commander of the British Empire!" I am so proud of what he has achieved. There are not many people who can go through life achieving so much without gaining some enemies along the way, but I can honestly say that that is exactly what Bill Baxter did.

Enough of this excruciating stuff – on with the story...

Chapter two – Discovery, spring 1991

"To get rich never risk your health. For it is the truth that
health is the wealth of wealth."
Richard Baker

Our first daughter, Katie was born in Brentford, Middlesex in
1987 and we then moved to a semi-detached house in
Prestwood, Bucks. Little Sophie followed three years later
and Ros gave birth to her in hospital in High Wycombe.
By this time, Baxter and Platts Ltd had been in business
for four years.

***

I was knackered and had fallen asleep in front of the
TV. When I opened my eyes and reached for the remote
control, I had a weird sensation in my right arm and hand,
sort of numb but with pins and needles. I didn't think
much more about it and went to bed.

When the alarm clock went off next morning, the first
thing I noticed was that the strange feeling was still there.
That day, sitting at my office desk in Chesham, I kept
taking my right shoe off as I was convinced my sock had
fallen down and that it was crumpled under the arch of
my foot. Each time I checked, I found that the sock was
not crumpled at all. The next day was a Saturday and I
rang Dad, and explained my symptoms. I said I thought it
was a trapped nerve – what did he think? Dad was his
usual caring but matter-of-fact self. 'I can't diagnose from
here. You are probably right, but go and see your GP and
get yourself checked.' Some years previously, when one of
my testicles had swollen to the size of a grapefruit, Dad's
take on the matter was, 'Not to worry, son. That's why the
good Lord gave you two.'

25

Discovery

My GP, Dr McKelvie, always inspired confidence. You knew she was interested and that she genuinely wanted to help. There was no question that for her, being a doctor was a vocation. By the time I got to see Dr McKelvie, I had allowed a great many medical possibilities to go through my mind, and had been busy trying to eliminate each one. Having recently met someone who was recovering from a brain tumour, this was, of course, right at the top of my list.

Dr McKelvie listened attentively while I explained the symptoms. Then she prodded me in various places with a needle and carried out a number of tests. I guessed these tests were all to do with mobility and co-ordination. 'This is a bit strange,' she said. 'It could be a trapped nerve, but it would have to be very high up the spinal column. I think maybe we should send you to see a neurologist.'

Dr McKelvie had a wonderful way of getting her patients to open up and she asked: 'What do you think it is? What is your biggest worry?'

'Could it be a brain tumour?'

'Unlikely, but possible.'

'Okay. Well I'd better see this neurologist then. When can I get an appointment?'

Dr McKelvie explained that there was a six-month waiting list.

'Hell's bells!' I said. 'Six months! I could be dead by then. What if it *is* a brain tumour?'

Dr McKelvie explained: 'Brain tumours are generally quite slow growing, and anyway, I really don't think that is what is wrong.'

'I have private medical insurance. Can I be seen any sooner?' I said.

She smiled. 'How would next Tuesday suit?'

Whilst this process was going on our business was flying. Our clients were mostly very large companies for whom we ran in-house catering services. Our expansion rate was mind-boggling, at over 40% a year. However, it had taken a while to get comfortably into profit.

By this time I think we employed about 150-200 people and operated 25 contracts, mostly in the South of England. The demands were phenomenal and we both felt the pressure, but Bill was probably better at hiding it than me.

When we started the company, we were convinced we could make good use of the new technology of computers. We wanted to be fully computerised in all that we did, and we tried to design things so that we did away with secretaries, and processed all accounting procedures with the minimum of human labour. Considering that we started the company with a total of £30,000, procured by re-mortgaging our homes, and that the state-of-the-art home computer then had only a 20 megabyte hard drive, we had given ourselves a bit of a hill to climb.

When it came time to produce our first invoice we were still running things out of one room in Bill's house in Prestwood, Buckinghamshire. We would spend all day talking to prospective clients, with Bill's cat occasionally walking across the desk or Daisy, his Dalmatian puppy, barking in the background. Not ideal for a supposedly professional catering company.

The day we produced our very first invoice was pretty fraught, as I struggled to get our newly configured accounting software to behave. I had spent weeks getting it ready, trying always to prepare for when our system would produce hundreds of invoices, not just one. It was past five o'clock in the afternoon, and I was about ready to get the system to print our very first invoice. Bill announced that if I didn't need him, he would do the vacuuming. He opened the stair cupboard and, while reaching for the vacuum, knocked the electricity supply off. All our work had gone - No such things as back-up drives in those days.

We worked all night and finally finished at eight the next morning. We just had time for a shave before heading off to present the invoice.

The day after seeing Dr McKelvie, I was parking at the office and, as I turned to the left to look over my shoulder, I noticed I was seeing double. This was a bit of a nuisance, but if I turned my body a bit more, or closed one eye, it was fine.

Later in the week the numbness had spread to the entire right side of my body.

I went off for the appointment with Dr Kaufman, a neurologist with bases in London and at my local private hospital in Great Missenden. Dr Kaufman is a calm and thoroughly nice chap; chatting with him was easy. He repeated all the tests Dr McKelvie had performed and carried out a number of others.

'What do you reckon then?' I said.

'Well, I have to say, I see many cases like yours, and quite often they come to nothing. It is quite likely you could walk away from here, things will get back to normal, and you'll never think about it again.'

While this was most comforting, I am very inquisitive by nature and, having a science background, I knew that something was not right and wanted to get to the bottom of it. I still couldn't get the idea of a brain tumour out of my mind, slow growing or not.

'What are the other options, then?' I asked.

'If you really want to proceed we would need to do a thing called an MRI scan [magnetic resonance imaging] of your brain,' Dr Kaufman replied. 'This will give us a really good set of pictures; images of slices through your brain and upper spinal column. It is an expensive procedure and the nearest place with an MRI machine is in the crypt of a church opposite the Planetarium in London.'

Discovery

Apparently, in those days the machines needed huge, heavy foundations and for some reason the crypt of this church was just right.

While not painful in any way, the MRI scan was unnerving. I was put on a fancy trolley and told to lie very still. The technicians then left the room and the trolley slid into a hole in the wall. The hole was like a tunnel and was not much wider than my shoulders. Inside this tunnel everything was white and claustrophobic. I was disorientated, as I had no sense of depth of vision. I was wearing earphones and occasionally the operator would issue commands such as, 'Very still now, please,' and then the machine would hum and throb, and bang loudly. The experience went on for about 45 minutes and I was told to make another appointment in one week's time to get the results.

When I entered his room a week later, Dr Kaufman was examining what looked like large x-rays.

'Well,' he said, and shuffled the pictures again. 'Well, I have to say that the MRI shows something, some areas of inflammation, but they are small and we are not certain of the diagnosis.'

'So what are the possibilities?' I asked.

Dr Kaufman paused for a moment. 'There are still a number of possibilities and I think it better that we do some more tests before I start going through all the possible causes. If you still want to carry on with the investigations, that is. Remember, you could still walk away from here and you may find you never need to come and see me again.'

Then I told him about the vision problems and that I just could not leave without hearing the truth. I know now that Kaufman knew exactly what was wrong with me, but he was also aware that the moment he made his diagnosis official would be the point when my life would change forever.

'We will need to admit you to hospital and carry out a procedure called a lumbar puncture,' he explained. 'In essence, this means we will take a sample of your spinal fluid. We can then use that to test for a number of diseases.'

It was about this time that I went to get up one morning and found I couldn't turn right. Having got both feet on the ground, I went to walk to the bedroom door but could only go left and unsteadily at that. This was completely weird. I was feeling a little nauseous, but I didn't fall over, I just couldn't go the way I wanted to go. I sat on the floor for a while and it was probably only minutes before I regained normal steering. I wasn't in pain, but this latest development was more than a little scary. I also felt a huge sense of inconvenience. I had work to do and this was in danger of getting in the way.

The next time I met Dr Kaufman I was lying on my side in a foetal tuck position, waiting to have a needle stuck in my spine. The procedure was actually simple and painless, and over in a few moments. I was warned that I shouldn't try to raise my head or get out of bed for 24 hours. Some hours later when I really needed to go to the toilet I did try briefly to raise my head from the pillow, thinking that maybe I would be all right. Instantly the most debilitating headache began. The severity of the pain was a horrible shock. Thankfully, as long as I stayed horizontal I was okay.

Twenty-four hours later I tried again to get out of bed, but it was like being hit by a tram, and in a fraction of a second, I went from feeling fine to feeling like my head was about to explode. Most lumbar punctures go off without a hitch, but apparently, a small number have complications. I stayed in hospital for five days.

Discovery

I was really worried now, and the fact that we had not got around to making our wills was bothering me. I called Bill's brother Richard, who is a solicitor, and asked him to draw up wills for Ros and me. We didn't have much to leave, but I wanted to make sure that what there was didn't just go to the solicitors for sorting things out. I felt I could die tidily now, and happy in the knowledge that my fishing rods would go to a good home!

On the third day the nurses tried to get me out of bed so that they could change the sheets. I explained again, that as soon as I left the horizontal, I was enormously uncomfortable, but they insisted I get up.

I was cross that the nurses didn't seem to understand, or perhaps they didn't believe me. In the end, I slipped out of bed and lay on the floor until they had finished. I was dreading having to leave the floor.

When I did get up to get back into bed, the headache started again. I was just getting settled back in bed when my neck muscles went into spasm. It felt as if I had been wired to the mains as every muscle in my neck rapidly contracted, relaxed and contracted again. I was trying to explain to the nurses but was in so much pain it was difficult to make myself understood.

At this point Dr Kaufman entered the room and immediately took charge. Very quickly I had small heated sandbags wrapped around my neck and Dr Kaufman gave me an injection of Valium. The pain and spasms subsided.

Composure regained, I said: 'You must know what it is by now, don't you? – I just want to know, am I going to die?'

Dr Kaufman looked shocked and said: 'Good heavens, I am sorry, I hadn't thought that you might be concerned about that. No, you are not going to die - you have Multiple Sclerosis.'

'Thank God for that,' I said, and then realised that was a pretty silly thing to say. Dr Kaufman went on: 'There is no easy way of giving this sort of news, but at least on this occasion I can soften the blow by assuring you that you are most definitely not about to die.'

I don't remember too much of the conversation from then on. I think my brain was overloaded and I was not really taking in much information after the headlines. Later, I found this was true for many people who have received this type of news. What I needed was for an expert to return within a day or so to explain the situation in more detail and to provide some perspective at an early stage.

It was precisely this experience which later made me so keen to support the idea of getting a specialist MS nurse for Guernsey.

Ros came to see me shortly after Dr Kaufman had delivered his verdict. It was difficult to discuss the situation with her meaningfully, because we both knew so little about the disease. In many ways, I think it was harder for her at that stage than for me. There we were, with a business that was taking off, but still a long way from being financially secure, with two young daughters and a huge mortgage. It must have seemed to Ros that the burden of all this was falling on her shoulders.

It didn't help when a few weeks later, she met the practice nurse who, trying to sympathise, but failing awfully, said: 'Oh Ros, it must be terrible to discover that you are no longer married to the man you thought you were married to.'

Ros has been my rock, and one of the worst things about my getting MS has been seeing the emotional strain the disease has placed on her.

She and I still laugh all the time and we seem to spark each other off. Humour has always been a great part of our family life. Both our daughters can be very funny and Katie in particular is a brilliant mimic and has a wicked sense of humour – dinner time with my family is my favourite time of day, not only because we all love our food, but mostly because it is so entertaining.

Ironically, a year before my diagnosis, Bill and I had been reviewing our insurances. We had chosen to take out key man, rather than critical illness, insurance. If we had chosen the latter, we would have had half a million pounds of security to ease the burden. I decided there was no point in worrying too much and gave myself a talking to. We were in a much stronger position than many who get this disease and, anyway, there was a good chance I would be able to work for years yet.

It was on about my third or fourth day in hospital that I asked Bill to bring a computer in so that I could carry on working. We had a number of important sales proposals to complete and I was getting bored with watching TV.

On the day before I was discharged, Bill came over and suggested we make a break for it and disappear for lunch to the local Chinese restaurant. I wasn't too sure about this, as the headaches, while much less severe, were still giving me grief. Bill is persuasive though, and said he had some stuff he wanted to chat about.

Over our meal we discussed the management of the news of my illness. It was hard to decide what to do, but in the end we decided not to make any sort of big announcement.

Bill and I were both anxious that the news shouldn't frighten clients, potential and existing, and we didn't want to unsettle our employees. We felt there wasn't actually much to say, anyway, as we had no way of knowing what the course of the disease would be. In the end, we decided on a low key but personal communication approach. This was a lot more work, but looking back on it, it was exactly this sort of approach that had made our company so successful.

I remember the last thing Bill said to me in that Chinese restaurant. 'No matter what happens, this is our business, and it will always remain that way. Also, Plattsy, nothing will stop us fishing together, even if I have to get you to the river bank in a wheelchair.'

I knew he meant every word, and for the first time since the diagnosis I felt some confidence creeping back. This must have been a difficult time for Bill and his family, as they too must have wondered if my illness would also change their lives.

The headaches returned with a vengeance that afternoon, but I wanted to get out of hospital, and decided not to say anything to the medics.

Two days later, I still had headaches and was feeling exhausted all the time. We had an important sales meeting to go to, where we were trying to persuade Lombard International to award us a catering contract at one of their offices.

Nick Howe, one of our area managers, put the front seat of his car down as far as it would go and we sped around the M25 with me almost horizontal. The client's consultants had heard that I had not been well and at the end of the meeting asked after my health. I was not about to lie or mislead and tried to give an honest, but perhaps optimistic, answer. We didn't get the contract and I have always wondered if it was that last question that sank our bid. We returned in the rush hour traffic around the motorway, with me horizontal again. I was washed out and when I arrived home Ros went mad, as apparently I was as white as a sheet and shaking. I decided to take it a bit easier but in just a day or two I was feeling much better.

Dr Kaufman had prescribed a course of steroids that are often effective in damping down the areas of inflammation in the brain associated with MS. Each day for a week I went off to the surgery to have the injection. Steroids are a wonder drug and not only did I feel physically better, but mentally I was on a real high too. I felt almost elated during this time, but that could just have been the disease itself, as such highs are well documented in cases of MS. Magically, the numbness and pins and needles slowly ebbed away.

It is said that it is at times like these that you find out who your friends are. I am not sure if that analysis is completely accurate. I think you discover new things about your friends and you find friends you didn't know you had.

I received many "get well" messages from people who I would previously have considered perhaps simply as acquaintances. While some of these could be described as courtesy messages, many had obviously spent time thinking about my family and me and they expressed genuine empathy for our situation.

At work, nothing much changed and, because I didn't look any different, I think people, for the most part, quickly forgot that I had MS. Sometimes MS is called the invisible disease because so many of the symptoms are not necessarily obvious to others. I was trying to learn how to live with the disease, and for me this was an active process. I have always been a "what if" type of person and Ros and I spent hours discussing how we would react if the disease progressed in certain ways.

I have to admit that both Ros and I ("Mr Uncertainty" himself) were having a hard time dealing with not knowing what our future might look like. Sometimes, I'd get to the point when I just couldn't discuss it anymore; realising that the reality was that discussion wasn't going to bring answers. But Ros gets comfort in talking and it was vital we both found a way through this.

Fish every Friday seemed more appealing now.

I wanted to be prepared, and I wanted Ros to be prepared, to cope with anything MS could throw at us. If there is a downside to this process, it is that it could be argued that we were worrying before we needed to.

This phenomenon of people forgetting I had the disease was also a bit strange to learn to live with. I never wanted sympathy and I definitely never wanted people to make allowances, but, just occasionally, and it seems silly and vain now, I wanted to be praised for the way I was coping.

I went back to see my GP and she gave me lots of useful information about MS, explaining that there were two main bodies that supported sufferers in the UK. The first and largest was the MS society, but locally, we had a very active branch of another organisation known as ARMS (Action and Research for MS).

The ARMS society had a well-resourced centre at an RAF base nearby. I went to the centre to have an assessment and so that they could explain all the work they did there. This was the first time I had met others with MS and it felt really strange and hard to accept, that I had a place amongst these people.

I was introduced to a very pretty girl called Violet. Violet could not walk and could hardly talk, but we managed to communicate, albeit slowly.

The last time I saw Violet, she was being delivered to the centre in the back of an estate car. The seats had been folded down and she lay on her side curled up, almost as if she was a baby. She could no longer communicate or move.

With infinite tenderness Violet's carer manoeuvred her so that she could get her from the car into a wheelchair. I was struck by the immense care and love Violet received from all around her. She could no longer participate in the activities in the centre, but her carers hoped that by at least going there every day, she would have some sense of continuity, some sense of normality in her life.

Discovery

If Violet could actually appreciate what was going on around her, then she would surely have taken some comfort from the love and respect her carers provided. My visits to the ARMS centre, while initially unsettling, were now actually uplifting and I looked forward to every session.

At the end of May I had the chance to help crew a sailing boat which the owner was selling and delivering to its new owner in Holland.

My friend Mike Dickson had invited me, but I hadn't met the owner or the rest of the crew before. We arranged to meet up in the yacht club bar at, I think, Chichester. We decided to have a meal before we boarded as the skipper said that because he was selling the boat, he had stripped it almost bare and there would be little to eat until we reached Holland.

Immediately we sat down to eat two of the crew began talking.

'Have you heard about Patricia?' said one.

'Oh God yes, isn't it awful?' the other replied. 'She was fine when I saw her six months ago; now what a change!' he continued.

'That's one disease I really never want to get – she's only 31, and now struck down with MS,' said the first.

I nearly fell off my seat. Talking earlier, Mike and I had decided not to say anything about my illness in case the skipper felt awkward about me coming along. Now here they were talking about MS and I really felt terrible about not saying something. I couldn't wait for the conversation to change.

It was an exhilarating trip and great fun. It was rough, though, and I was cold all the time. We had very little sleep and I had spent much of the voyage on the edge of being sick. Strangely perhaps, for someone who loves the sea and boats so much, I have always suffered from seasickness, but usually I am sick once and then can get

on with things. For a while, I even had the nickname of
"One Chuck Rob".

This time, the sickness didn't completely disappear
when I reached dry land. Occasionally I was getting a
feeling that I suppose is best described as vertigo. It was
like that horrid feeling you get when you are standing
looking over a cliff, or the top of a tall building. I kept
getting an almost irresistible urge to get as low as
possible. This was happening once or twice a day, but
generally the feeling was fairly short-lived.

At this time, we were negotiating to buy a new house.
We had fallen in love with an old flint-built cottage
around the corner from our Edwardian semi on the busy
main road in Prestwood. I had a really good feeling about
our new house. While I never said anything to Ros, and
having a science background, I tend to be very sceptical
about such things; I took the fact that the master bedroom
was on the ground floor almost as some sort of omen. This
room was lovely and looked, through period windows,
into the small garden on two sides. One side was shaded
by an enormous cherry tree and on the other, French
windows opened on to the small lawn. I felt comfortable
in the knowledge that if mobility became a problem, at
least I would not have to worry about negotiating stairs to
get to bed.

This was a stressful time, as we struggled to sell our
house and raise the funds we needed for the new place.
House prices generally were in decline and buyers were in
short supply. Eventually we did find a buyer for our
house, but the sale almost fell through when he failed to
entirely raise mortgage he needed to meet our asking
price. We had already reduced the price to well below
what we had paid five years earlier and we couldn't bring
ourselves to reduce it further. Instead, I came up with the
idea of lending our buyers the last £1,500 they needed to
complete the deal. They agreed to this and the sale went

ahead. On the day of the move I was sorting things in our new kitchen and the vertigo feeling suddenly struck me. The feeling was so strong I immediately had to sit on the floor.

Slowly, over weeks, it became worse. Then one night I woke feeling hot and sweaty with a sort of buzzing in my head; it was 3am. My eyes started to flick quickly and uncontrollably to one side before returning and then flicking back, over and over again. Very quickly I was dizzy to the point of nausea, and I was frightened.

It was like being on a sickening fairground ride which you can't get off. After about an hour, things subsided but I was exhausted.

The next night I woke again, precisely at 3am. This time fortunately, there was no eye flicking. However, the buzzing in my head had been replaced with what felt like waves of pressure and anxiety. Each wave took about a minute to build to an excruciating crescendo before subsiding.

These waves went on for about 40 minutes. The same thing happened the next night, and the next night, and the next.

Ros, herself very frightened, tried to comfort me during these episodes, but I had to ask her to leave me to get on with it. I just couldn't deal with this and prevent her from being scared. The saga went on night after night.

During these attacks I was completely white and very clammy. My stomach churned and gurgled loudly. While it was happening I really couldn't do much other than sit or lie on the floor, sweating and swearing profusely, and wait for it to subside.

Dr Kaufman tried all sorts of drugs, including many treatments for sea-sickness but nothing made any difference. Finally, Dr Kaufman decided to try me on an anti-epilepsy drug called Tegretol. This lessened the severity of the symptoms, but did not stop them.

Discovery

For the next seven years the attacks continued, mostly at night, but then they started to occur during the day. I could never tell when it would happen next.

Our business was flourishing, and work was hectic. I found I was exhausted most of the time. Things became acute when I started to have these episodes shortly after having fallen asleep. That meant I didn't dare fall asleep in front of the TV, or even take an afternoon nap, for fear of triggering an attack. It became a vicious mental torture, as I desperately needed more sleep, but was to terrified to close my eyes.

I kept increasing the dosage of Tegretol in order to curb the attacks at night.

Eventually I was at the maximum amount allowed and I knew I was becoming mentally much slower than I used to be. I felt sluggish and, to an extent, I felt life had lost some of its shine.

Normally I am interested and inquisitive about everything around me, but now work and life generally seemed a bit dull and more like hard work than fun. Ros was constantly on at me to slow down, work shorter hours, and make allowances for the fact that I was ill. That, to me, was to give in.

We had huge rows on the subject, which led to even more stress. I just kept assuring Ros that I wouldn't have to work like this forever and that it would all turn out for the best in the end. Ros coped for a long time, but I know that through the effects of the disease and the drugs, I was becoming less communicative, which was difficult for Ros because she desperately needed the therapy that our communicating bought to her.

Everyone had a breaking point. For Ros, it was when she discovered Katie was being bullied at school. Ros slid into depression.

Instead of being the bubbly, funny little Welsh girl I had fallen in love with, she was now just now heartbreakingly sad. Because of the drugs, I wasn't feeling many emotions at all, but even through my drug haze, I knew she needed help. But, who to turn to? Who would understand what our family was going through, and who could see the effect that MS was having on us all? There was no MS nurse to help us.

What was so difficult was that Ros couldn't see the change in herself. I think she just thought her feelings and her continual weeping were a natural part of what life had dealt her; she couldn't see that she, too, was now ill. Although it took us many years to realise it, Katie suffered mental scars through this time which stayed with her until she was in her 20s.

Finally, I managed to persuade Ros to make an appointment with her doctor. Ros was prescribed anti-depressants and offered counselling. By the time she took up the offer of counselling, a few weeks had gone by and a little of her normal sparkle was returning. She came back from the first session and said: 'It's all bollocks and he's a twat. I'm not going back.' I started to hope that my little Welsh dragon was on her way back from the edge of doom.

***

In the 10th year of our being in business and six years after my MS had been diagnosed, Bill and I had an offer for the company. We had had many approaches before, but, unlike the others, this one was difficult to ignore.

We had become very successful. By this time we employed almost 2,000 people and produced and served over 30,000 meals a day in 150 locations around the country. The company had won all the top awards our industry had to offer and I suppose we were *the* name in contract catering at that time.

Discovery

After we had initially told the prospective buyer not to bother us any more, shrewdly, he challenged us to name our price.

Years before, Bill and I had talked fancifully about our exit price, and we agreed we wouldn't sell until we could bank an amount of money that should guarantee a comfortable retirement. We first had this discussion in the very early days of our business and of course at that time it was a flight of fancy. It was difficult to believe that now we could have actually reached that point. I don't think either of us really wanted to sell the company.

Bill, particularly, found a huge thrill in the cut and thrust of the business. I was finding it more difficult not to allow MS to affect my business life, and was worried that things might rapidly deteriorate, but I didn't really want to sell our baby to anyone.

Also, Bill and I had a unique working relationship – we really enjoyed working together and I didn't want that to finish. In the end, for both of us there was an element within the decision making of banking some money while we could. It was now starkly obvious to us both that no one can predict the future and it seemed to make sense to grab some security while we had that opportunity.

Bill wasn't even 40 at that point and he knew he had a good chance of doing it all over again. Perhaps, for once in my life I opted for a degree of certainty.

Throughout my career I was almost obsessive about punctuality and preparation, while Bill would be far more laid back. When going to a business meeting I always drove, as, although Bill is a much better driver than me (he was a karting champion in his youth), he went much faster than I could cope with. So I drove, and he slept.

With this obsession about punctuality I was therefore distraught when I had a couple of terrible lapses of memory. At the time I thought I had just made a mistake, but I accept now that the disease and the drugs were at least partly responsible.

The worst of these lapses was when I completely forgot about a sales meeting with the UK Managing Director of Daewoo cars. Our sales director, Mike Smith, had put in a shed-full of work wooing Daewoo and on this day I was meant to meet him and the MD at one of our contracts to try to seal the deal.

When I received the call from Mike asking where I was, my heart went through the floor. Unusually for a salesman, Mike never was much good at lying, and when he simply told the MD of Daewoo that I had forgotten, the latter was understandably furious and we lost the opportunity of doing business with Daewoo.

Bill and I came to the uneasy decision to accept our buyer's offer and we started the difficult and somewhat underhand business known as "due diligence". This involved proving to our buyer that we were worth buying at the agreed price and that we had no skeletons in our corporate closet. The hard part was that we had to do this without letting anyone else know that we were contemplating selling.

Of course, many of our employees noticed Bill and I now often had our doors closed, which was highly unusual, and that we both often suddenly had to go to non-specific meetings together. Amazingly, most of the people who noticed our strange behaviour reckoned we were about to buy another company, not the other way around.

We sold the company to Granada in 1997 and agreed to stay on as joint managing directors for a one-year earn-out period.

The attacks had started to happen more frequently during the day. I had a number at work, but managed to cover these by asking not to be disturbed and closing my door. These symptoms were so strange that I started to wonder if I did in fact have MS, or whether it was some other disease.

My neurologist had never heard of symptoms exactly the same as mine and thought it worth investigating further. Dr Kaufman sent me off to the National Epilepsy Centre where, coincidentally, Baxter and Platts were the caterers. It was strange to be entering this place as a patient rather than a supplier.

The employees at the centre were amazing and very reassuring. There were plenty of jokes about the food my company served them on a daily basis and they made me feel at ease. I had lots of wires stuck to my head with superglue and they recorded my brain activity for about half an hour. This first test was normal, so they decided to hook me up to a portable monitor and record things for 24 hours.

I left the centre with about 20 different coloured wires glued to my scalp. All the wires were gathered behind my head like an electronic mane and these then joined up to a box which I was to wear at my side. I had very recently taken delivery of a new company car, which was a convertible, and I took a perverse pleasure in driving home from the centre with the roof down. People looked on with a mixture of horror and intrigue as if I was some sort of modern day Frankenstein's monster.

The 24-hour test suggested I didn't have epilepsy and I went back to Dr Kaufman to see if he had any other ideas.

Things were now very bad and I was desperate to know if these were symptoms of MS or whether they might be from some other cause that might be treatable.

Dr Kaufman suggested I go back into hospital for more tests. His idea was to take me off the drugs and monitor me while I was actually having one of the episodes. I didn't relish the thought of doing that, but looked forward to being a step closer to some answers. At 3am on the first night of my re-admittance to hospital I woke with an episode about to start. I pressed the buzzer as instructed and a nurse came rushing into the room. She turned white at the sight of me: eyes rolling, deathly pale, and cursing loudly with the discomfort.

Within minutes the room was full of nurses and doctors performing various tests. Now that I was off the drugs, the attack was a bad one - horrendous. I couldn't stop my eyes rolling and the sound of my stomach churning could be heard above the clamour of all those around me.

I had become used also to these episodes being accompanied with a strange odour – a smell of rotting flesh. This time, the smell was so powerful it made me want to retch. I was later told that no one else could smell anything strange.

The next day, the nurse who had come into the room first the previous evening, said she was convinced I was dying. Dr Kaufman came to talk to me about the results of all the tests. I was rather hoping that he was going to tell me that I had some exotic disease and that it was curable.

Of course this wasn't what he said: he just confirmed that Multiple Sclerosis was the devil that was tormenting me. His best guess was that the disease was affecting my temporal lobe, and this was certainly suggested by the scan results.

The symptoms of MS are often wide-ranging and this is because the disease can affect any part of the central nervous system. It started in quite a conventional way in my case, but rather rarer symptoms have developed since. Some sufferers initially show mild symptoms, then the disease progresses quickly to the point where they have perhaps lost mobility, speech and even sight.

The MS Society has decided that the term "sufferer" is not politically correct – well, excuse me, but the minute we all stop suffering, I will stop using the term. This rapidly deteriorating variant is known as primary progressive MS.

Others can show symptoms that almost completely disappear for weeks, months or even years, before the disease shows again. When MS shows in this way it is known as relapsing-remitting MS.

It is also possible for relapsing remitting MS to develop into the progressive form of the disease, known as secondary progressive MS.

Ros and I had thought about retirement after my earn-out period and had given a lot of thought to where we might go, as staying in Buckinghamshire, so far away from the sea, was not an option.

Languishing in bed in hospital, I realised that it was crazy that I was trying to complete the earn-out year while being so unwell. I spoke to Bill to see what his reaction would be to me going a couple of months early, although I already knew I had his support. The chaps at Granada were very obliging and after a brief discussion they agreed that I need not return to work. This probably suited them well, as, to be honest, I was not an ideal employee and never really got used to being one, after 10 years of owning the company.

Chapter three - To Guernsey

There is nothing like a dream to create the future.
Victor Hugo

We made the decision to move to Guernsey. Obviously there were tax advantages to the move, but more than anything we felt we needed a complete change of lifestyle. I had a feeling that stress probably had a lot to do with my MS and, if we stayed in England, I knew I would find it hard not to go back to work. Ros too, felt she needed a new start and, as much as we loved our little flint cottage and our close friends and family in England, we sensed we couldn't have a fresh start if we stayed. Our daughters, Katie and Sophie, were very excited about the new house and we hoped they would soon fall in love with the island, given the new experiences and freedom Guernsey would offer them.

My first taste of Guernsey[1] had come when, as a boy of 11, I was given the Shell Channel pilot book that described all the harbours and ports of the English Channel. By far the most exotic and alluring of these was St Peter Port. The picture of the harbour entrance, and the dire warnings about the difficulty of the navigation, are another memory which thankfully escaped the holes in my Swiss cheese memory. I promised myself that one day I would sail through that harbour entrance.

It was some 20 years later that I first set foot in the island. I was sailing with friends in a yacht we had

---

[1] Guernsey is one of the half-dozen inhabited Channel Islands. They are part of the British Isles but not of the United Kingdom or European Union. The Bailiwick (administrative area) of Guernsey contains the island of Guernsey itself plus Alderney, Sark and Herm. Strangely, the islands are not technically in the English Channel at all; they are, in fact, in the Bay of St Malo. Guernsey is 20 miles west of France and 80 miles south of England.

chartered from Poole, and the plan had actually been to head for Jersey.

Halfway across the channel the barometer started to drop, the wind speed increased and it became obvious the weather forecast we had received before we set off was wrong.

Most of the crew were on deck, but my good mate Phil Robertson was down below navigating. I was in my preferred place – at the helm, where, like driving a car rather than being a passenger, I am less susceptible to seasickness. Phil, on the other hand, could stay down below in atrocious weather and even smoke a cigar without feeling the slightest bit queasy.

As we reached the infamous Alderney Race[2], the wind was gusting near gale force, and we knew we were in for a bit of a battering. We had thought diverting into Alderney but still there was general consensus that we should push on.

Phil's head appeared in the hatchway and, as he cheerfully asked, 'Anyone for a cuppa?' we were hit by a massive double wave. Phil was thrown across the cabin. As the boat violently corrected, he was then thrown across to the other side.

For a short while, there was no sign of life or sound from below. I was fighting with helm and all on deck were shocked and hanging on with bloodless knuckles, looking to see if we were going to be knocked flat by another wave. We called to Phil, but he didn't answer - then he appeared and slowly made his way into the cockpit without making a sound. He turned white before our eyes and was obviously in great pain and at first, was unable to speak.

Phil had landed heavily on the stove and we suspected that he had cracked some ribs. The crew helped him below

---

[2] The Alderney Race is the stretch of water between Alderney and the French coast. The swift tidal currents and rocky undulating nature of the sea bed often produce confused and dangerous overfalls.

again and tried to make him comfortable but the constant angry motion of the boat was aggravating his pain immensely. We needed to get Phil to hospital and decided to abandon our plans to get to Jersey. We dosed Phil with painkillers and changed course for Guernsey, which was 20 miles closer than Jersey.

Three hours later, Phil was a little more comfortable and we were sailing through the pier heads of St Peter Port. There was a particular magic for me to see the lighthouse at the end of the Southern pier head appear. I was completing an ambition to sail to Guernsey which I had held ever since I was a young lad and had seen that grainy black and white picture of that lighthouse in the pilot book.

We rushed Phil to the island's hospital. The doctor confirmed he'd cracked some ribs but, other than give Phil some stronger painkillers, there was no other treatment needed. We were storm-bound for three days, which gave us an opportunity to explore the island in some detail and for Phil to mend a little before we set sail again.

We hired a small minibus and embarked on a cultural and gastronomic tour of Guernsey. It was pouring with rain when we called in at Blind O'Reilly's pub in St Sampson's. Guernsey folk will now be laughing that I might follow a sentence about culture and gastronomy by talking about Blind O'Reilly's, but trust me, humour is at the very heart of the culture of the island.

The pub's roof couldn't keep up with the downpour and was leaking in places. Buckets were placed at strategic points to catch the drips, and customers were using these buckets as ashtrays. The resulting yellow liquid in the buckets looked revoltingly like something else. But nothing could dampen the humour and when the barmaid came to ask if we were comfortable, crew mate Roger Kern, famous for his dry wit, pointed to the bucket and quipped, 'Yes thanks, we've all been.'

To Guernsey

You probably had to have been there, and to have been the stomach side of a few pints of Guinness, to appreciate how bizarrely funny this was, but the barmaid fell about and we were left chuckling for days afterwards.

Being a caterer and a keen cook, I suppose I'm a bit of a food critic, so I was blown away by the standard and variety of food on offer in the scores of eateries on the island. The scallops served in the Café de Moulin (unfortunately now closed) were incredible and we had such an enjoyable meal that lunch stretched into dinner. We didn't have a bad or even mediocre meal during our stay. I was seriously impressed.

Despite the terrible weather, I don't think we stopped laughing all the time we were there. Guernsey's spell worked on me from the start and I felt very comfortable - almost as if I already knew the place. At that time of course, I had no idea that I might one day have the chance to live there.

Once we'd sold the business, Ros and I had to give some serious thought to where we were going to base ourselves. We both wanted to be near the sea and I suspected that if I stayed in Buckinghamshire, the temptation to get involved with business might be too strong to resist. Our decision was helped along by our solicitor who gave us a list of places we could choose to move to. The money we received from the sale of the business was probably all the money we would ever have, so a favourable tax rate was important. But tax was by no means the main consideration. This was going to be a major change for us, and would mean taking our little girls out of the school they loved. We also knew we should perhaps be prepared for this move to be our last.

Guernsey was of course on the list given to us by the solicitor. We considered other places, but some, for instance Monaco, were a bit flash for us, or others, such as the Caribbean, we considered to be too far away from friends and family.

Ros was happy to visit Guernsey and, on our first trip, the lovely Shona from Swoffers estate agents showed us some properties. At first we were very dispirited. I'd given Shona a budget to work to, but I hadn't realised that property in Guernsey was so expensive. By about the third house, Ros, never one for holding back, refused even to view the interior and gave a clearer brief to Shona. Shona responded saying, 'If you double your budget I'm sure I can find you something you will like.'

At the time, this was an unbelievable amount of money, but we rationalised that in the overall scheme of things it was do-able. So, we agreed and arranged a second trip.

Shona called a week or so later saying she had a number of properties she would like us to view, including one in particular she had a feeling we would like.

The last house we saw that day was the one Shona was confident about, and she was right; we fell instantly in love with a big old farmhouse in the parish of St Andrew's. The girls loved it too, but it was such a lot of money I had to go away and do some serious maths. After all, I didn't want us to be living on rabbits and blackberries again.

***

To Guernsey

Grandad's Green Flash

At sunset, you'd stand on the beach, in that same pose,
quietly, with a steady face,
looking to the horizon and slowly smoothing
and stroking your stubbly grey beard, as the colours and
warmth of the day drained back to the sea.

You used to say you were waiting for the sun to sizzle on
the sea and flash green,
but even when we were tiny,
we knew it was something else.

In those moments we sensed that we were losing you.

***

We bought that old farmhouse in the centre of the island in the parish of St Andrew's.

Although St Andrew's is the only parish that doesn't have a coast, the island is only eight miles by three and nowhere is more than a couple of miles from the sea.

We moved into our new home in 1998. We quickly found a new and large circle of friends, mostly through meeting the parents of our daughters' friends from school.

The island is a magical place to live. The people are very welcoming, there is little crime and it is very safe. The pace of life is as slow as you want it to be and there is a lot to do.

I will always resist typecasting a race or a people – after all, that's the basis of much prejudicial discrimination in the world and ultimately the stuff of wars. Having said that, I did sense a different, perhaps generally more positive and "can do" attitude, from people living in Guernsey. Guerns (as residents have become known in recent years) seem more likely to throw themselves into everything with vigour, and never miss an opportunity to celebrate; they also appreciate what they have, and are fiercely and rightly proud of their island.

On my first visit to our local garage the chap behind the counter was welcoming, but he also made sure I knew my place. 'You will find us very friendly but you will also discover that you will never truly become one of us. If you have a son who is born here, he won't be considered a Guern, nor will his son. It probably won't be until your great-grandson, is born here that the Platts family will be accepted as Guernsey – nothing against you personally,' he said, 'It's just the way it is.'

This was a bit unsettling, as our family really wanted to adopt and be adopted by the island. Garage hands aside, most Guernsey folk welcomed us and every member of the Platts family threw themselves into island life.

The proportion of born-and-bred Guernsey people in the population has declined somewhat as the finance industry has grown and employed more and more workers from off the island, mainly from England. A new acquaintance's name was often the first clue that this person might be locally born. Many Guernsey names stem from French families and will often sound French or are preceded by "Le". Underlining the welcome feeling we had from the Island, little Sophie came home from a shopping trip with Ros one day saying that she thought the people in Guernsey had "smiling disease".

We had decided to be open about my illness with our daughters. Ros wasn't sure how much to shield from them, but they are both very bright, and I felt we should just be truthful if they asked questions. Ros has a wonderful way with the girls and is always in tune with their moods, their needs and with the all the latest fashions. This is a great attribute but it is a double-edged sword sometimes, as when they have a problem, she feels their pain as if it is her own.

To Guernsey

With Katie, our eldest, I tried to be matter-of-fact about the subject and I suppose it was over months that she learnt all about MS. This way, I don't think it was a shock.

Even so, if I was suffering "an episode" I would disappear into my bedroom and the girls would be told that Daddy was having a bit of a turn and not to disturb him.

There is no doubt that MS has affected their lives, but the effect would have been much greater if I had not been able to carry on working, or if I had lost mobility or sight or speech. I know both girls have worried that the disease will progress and that their Dad might suffer any of these problems, but as time went on, and as they matured, I think these possibilities came to trouble them less.

When I was diagnosed, the ARMS people gave me all sorts of leaflets and I gave one to Katie that was designed with youngsters in mind. It felt strange giving my daughter a leaflet especially, as I recall, the only leaflet my Dad ever gave me when I was young was about sex education.

He chose to give me a leaflet rather than speak to me because he, or possibly I, was too embarrassed to have a conversation. I think the title was something like "Now you are a man". I suppose the equivalent today would be called "Janet and John get it on".

Anyhow, I didn't want Katie to think that MS was something I wouldn't talk about and therefore made a point of discussing the leaflet with her. Some years later, when she was 12, she chose MS as the subject of a special project at school and spent some time researching the subject on the Internet.

One morning I nearly spluttered my cornflakes over the breakfast table as she asked, quite matter-of-factly, 'Dad, can you tell me, please – are you impotent and are you also incontinent?'

To Guernsey

Although generally the girls found the idea of their father's MS easier to deal with as time went on, Sophie, who was only one when I was diagnosed, still gets upset whenever I have the slightest thing wrong with me and always worries that the latest ailment, be it a headache or a cold, could be the onset of a relapse.

Katie, who is now a doctor herself, cites her dad's MS as a major reason for choosing medicine as a career.

My brother, my two sisters and I have all caused our parents our fair share of worry one way and another. I know my mother used to feel guilty, as she blames the genes on her side of the family for my condition, because her father had MS. This, of course, is nonsense, as it is not an inheritable disease. There is, however, what is known as a familial tendency. In other words, if a close relative has the disease you are more likely than average to also get the disease, but the chance is still small. I had other things in common with my Grandad. He too was a caterer.

As a young man learning his craft, he worked at the Shepherd hotel in Cairo, the Strand Palace and the Berkeley, some of the finest hotels in the world.

Grandad was a very dapper dresser, witty and charming and, before he retired, was always immaculately presented. At the age of 32 he enlisted in the RAF and worked as ground crew during the Second World War.

My mother and my uncle were among a relatively small number of children evacuated to Canada to escape the nightly bombings of the City of London. The British government stopped these evacuations following the horrifying torpedoing of the ship City of Benares with 400 souls on board, 100 of who were children.

To send your children so far away must have been an appallingly difficult decision to make and was one that was to scar my mother and her brother for life. My mother didn't see or talk to her parents for five years.

To Guernsey

Grandad later went to Germany as a part of the occupying forces and saw at first hand the devastation of Dresden. This changed him, and he returned a bitter and cynical man. Our family now wonders if the stress of what he experienced in Germany might have contributed to the onset of his MS.

Later, he became one of the first catering managers at Heathrow airport, which at that time was little more than a collection of Nissen huts.

Grandad was often poorly. Before the war, he had developed pneumonia and almost died. Mum remembers many days when he was at home complaining of not being well, but she doesn't remember many specific symptoms. She does remember that when she was out walking with him, he would sometimes stop and blink, and she now thinks perhaps he was suffering from double vision.

His wealthy great Aunt Agnes died and left him £1,000 – a considerable sum in those days. With this, he moved into a large house and leased a restaurant in Wimbledon.

His health deteriorated and he started to slow up and become confused. When my Nan insisted he went to his doctor to be checked out, his G.P. noticed his strange gait. The doctor may have suspected MS and did in fact send him to the Atkinson Morley hospital for a lumbar puncture. The tests could not have confirmed MS, as instead, the diagnosis was early senile dementia. Grandad was then 56.

My mother became very involved in the local branch of the Alzheimer's Society and spent years raising awareness and funds for the cause. In those days, it was not possible to diagnose MS with certainty and poor old Grandad went to his grave with all around him believing he had Alzheimer's. It was only after the post mortem that we discovered he had MS.

I have very few memories of Grandad and only really recall him being rather frail and that from time to time he would disappear, only to turn up a while later in the back of a police car, having been found wandering, lost and confused. I do worry about ending up as he did, but then again, he lived comfortably and in his last few years was probably not really aware that he was ill.

The waves in my head continued to plague me and now this was joined by a new ailment, itching. My skin itched all over. My scalp itched, my groin itched, and I scratched at my forearms so much that they bled. I tried all sorts of lotions and creams but nothing worked. 'This surely cannot be MS,' I thought. I did some research on the Internet and found reference to just this problem on an American site. Itching is another symptom of MS, but it is not common. I went to see my doctor in Guernsey and he agreed with what I had discovered and prescribed an antihistamine that thankfully controlled the itching problem.

Our first few months on the Island were frenetic while we repaired, redecorated and rearranged the house. I found these tasks helpful in not letting me dwell too much on what was going on at Baxter & Platts. When I did find myself thinking about the life I had just left, I had very mixed and confused emotions. Back in England I was somebody, I had a past, I had a successful business and I suppose I had a place in the world. In Guernsey, I was nobody.

When people asked, 'And what do you do?' I found it very difficult to say that I was retired. When I did admit to not being employed, it was a complete conversation stopper.

Sometimes, I had the feeling that people found this answer somewhat distasteful, almost as if they were thinking 'lazy sod should get a job'. I didn't want to get into the "I've got MS" thing as soon as I met someone new. Anyway, the fact that I had MS was not the whole reason why I wasn't working, but this was all too complicated, and I felt it unnecessary to explain at a first meeting. I didn't want this to be my label now. I didn't want MS to define me.

On the other hand, I was terribly excited about our new island life. The Island is only 24 square miles but it packs a lot in. A bit like Dr Who's Tardis, it seems much bigger and busier from the inside.

I am by nature an adventurer, an explorer and an enquirer. I like doing things which are new to me and I like to find out how things work. If there is a small element of risk or indeed an element of skill to a new adventure, there is no doubt that I will enjoy it more. It is a shame that most of the great physical adventures, explorations and challenges of the world have already been completed. It is also a shame that this disease will stop me doing some things that I wanted to do. I wanted to sail across the Atlantic single-handed, I wanted to do at least one leg of a round-the-world race. I would love to have sailed in the South Atlantic.

Of course, it is not the disease stopping me directly, but the presence of the disease means my family would have to endure heightened and unreasonable worry if I was to insist on trying to do these things. I also have to be honest and admit I am now a little more frightened of trying these challenges because I am concerned that the disease might in some way affect my abilities. I often console myself, however, with the thought, when I have completed some small challenge or adventure, that while it may not be a world first, it is still a first for me.

One reason I found the sailor and explorer Tristan Jones particularly inspiring was because he made up his own challenges all the time. When thinking what great sailing adventure he might undertake he was at first a bit despondent. He realised, you see, that someone had already sailed around the world single-handed, around the world non-stop, across the Atlantic, around the world backwards, and so on.

Jones took a leap of lateral (or perhaps more correctly vertical) thinking when he decided to sail in the lowest and highest waters of the world. His adventures sailing in Lake Titicaca and in the Dead Sea are now legendary.

As the house neared completion, I found other things keeping me busy. Sophie, my youngest daughter, had expressed a desire to learn to sail and she was certainly in the right place to do that. I became very involved with the local sailing club and in teaching kids to sail. Sophie quickly became very proficient in her tiny Optimist dinghy. Within a year, we were travelling to England or France or Jersey every couple of months so that Sophie could take part in yet another regatta.

Ros and I placed an order for a boat of my own, to be built by a local yard. We decided we should buy a motor boat, as the very strong tides around the Channel Islands make sailing a less than convenient method of getting from A to B. Specifying all the hundreds of widgets, gadgets and systems for the boat kept me busy, challenged and amused for weeks.

In among some other boxes I wanted to tick was one labelled "learn to fly". Ros had bought me introductory flying lesson years ago, but I had been too busy to make use of the voucher and I am ashamed to say it went out of date before I eventually got around to try to make use of it. Getting on and off Guernsey can sometimes be difficult. For some, escaping island life even for a day or two is an absolute necessity. I had it in my mind that, if I learnt to fly, perhaps I could join a syndicate and share a small plane. Apart from being a thrill, being able to fly would give us great freedom.

I presented myself at the Guernsey flying club. 'I've come to learn to fly,' I said, by way of introduction to a chap whose epaulettes and a moustache certainly made him look every inch a pilot.

'Great to have you along old chap – take a seat. I'm afraid we'll have to get the boring paperwork out of the way first. Have you been to see the quack for your medical yet?' he asked.

'I'm sorry, no, I didn't know I had to have one,' I replied.

I was really naïve – of course you have to have a medical. I was so blinkered by the excitement of actually getting into a plane that I hadn't given the health side a thought.

'Yes, we will need a medical certificate. There is one doctor in the Island who is registered with the Civil Aviation Authority to issue such certificates. I don't suppose a strapping chap like you will have any problem though,' he said.

'Well actually', I said, 'I might have a problem, as I have MS.' The pilot's next statement was one I had heard so many times before, I could sense it coming 'Really?' he said, 'I'd have never guessed - you look so well.'

A few days after seeing the doctor, I was disappointed to receive a pink slip from the Civil Aviation Authority (CAA) effectively banning me from flying solo. I had heard of people climbing back into the cockpit only months after having a heart attack, so I was surprised at this outright and non-negotiable ban. When I had seen the doctor I had protested that I was very fit (I used to do two or three five-mile runs a week then) and that I didn't consider my symptoms at the moment should prevent me from flying. The doctor explained that MS was a condition proscribed by the CAA and under no circumstances would it allow an affected person to fly solo.

After this, I decided to take a leaf out of Tristan Jones's book and realised if I couldn't get the thrill of going flying,

I too should think vertically. I could perhaps tick off another box, the one labelled "learn to dive".

We had had a small 'try dive' on holiday one year and, when I suggested we could go off somewhere hot and learn to dive, the girls were really excited. Ros was excited with the 'somewhere hot' bit, but because she had ear problems, she wouldn't be learning to dive.

Before mentioning anything, I had been to my GP to see if my health would be an issue. 'I think you'll be fine.' he said. 'After all, they use barometric pressure to treat some MS sufferers. You never know, you might actually do yourself some good!'

So now, Katie, Sophie and I are all advanced divers and we grab every opportunity we can to go exploring under the sea. This new-found skill has been useful on a number of occasions when I have needed to clear a line from a propeller or inspect the hull of a boat.

In June 1998 I flew to our neighbouring island of Alderney in order to rendezvous with friends Malcolm and Lindy Robertson – a couple we had met a few years before while on a flotilla sailing holiday in Turkey. Malc and Lindy were on the first leg of a world trip in their 45ft steel yacht *Mr Bean* and I had offered to meet them in Alderney and help them navigate the tricky approach to Guernsey. There's an old adage that you can count the number of your real friends on the fingers of one hand, well for Ros and me and the girls, Malc and Lindy were definitely two of those digits.

We'd got on like a house on fire during that Turkish holiday and had remained firm friends. To the girls, Malc and Lindy were like an aunt and uncle. Shortly after I was diagnosed with MS, Malcolm discovered he had bladder cancer and while he was having treatment, he and Lindy had visited us at our Flint Cottage in Prestwood.

During their visit, Malc and I had a conversation which started off by us comparing our initial reactions, him to being told he had cancer and me to being told I had MS. I was fascinated with Malc's response. I suppose I shouldn't have been surprised that his reaction might differ from mine as, after all, he was facing a possibly terminal illness, whereas people rarely die from MS.

Malc was consumed with the idea that he must experience as much as he could in life while he still had time. In a way, although I consider myself a positive person, I worried the opposite might be true and that I might find the possibility of living with a progressive disease for perhaps 40 years might just be too much.

Malc, a successful entrepreneur who had built his father's bakery business in Hastings, now had a thriving chain of bakery and *Mr Bean* cafe operations. Fortunately, with the support of their four children, who at one stage all worked in the business, he and Lindy were in a situation where they could afford to take long periods away from the coalface.

I liked Malc for all sorts of reasons. I liked the fact that he took up sailing relatively late in life but didn't see this as any hindrance to taking on the most adventurous of voyages. I liked the way he planned things in his life and I was flattered when he consulted me about plans for his business or his sailing adventures. More than anything perhaps, I had great empathy for his dreams. Lindy is an attractive woman, very open and easy to get on with and she has a wicked sense of humour. Sailing around the world was Malc's dream, not Lindy's, but as they progressed Lindy joined in ownership of the dream more and more. As a couple they were incredibly good hosts and great fun.

Malcolm had laser treatment to remove the cancer and was told he had to return regularly for check-ups. The prognosis for his condition was good, as the cancer hadn't spread and the specialists were confident that it could be kept under control. I caught up with Malc and lindy as planned, and had an exciting 20-mile sail from Alderney back to Guernsey.

Their boat Mr Bean was a very sturdy steel-built, Bruce Roberts-designed, cutter rigged sloop. She was heavy and consequently not fast. Her sheer mass helped her, though, to shrug off the swirling and confused waters of the Alderney race, almost elbowing her way through the water, and I immediately felt that Malc and Lindy had bought the right boat for the job.

They stayed with us for a few days, making final preparations for the first long passage of their circumnavigation. Their next port of call after Guernsey was to be La Coruña in northern Spain, approximately 500 miles away. Their passage plan took them west of Ushant and then straight across the notorious Bay of Biscay.

I was particularly interested in this plan, as a Biscay crossing was something I hoped to do myself one day and I had already read a great deal about this most challenging of ocean voyages.

Mr Bean, and her relatively novice crew, left Guernsey with the sun shining and a good north-westerly breeze to help her on her way. They hoped to make landfall 5 days later. Unfortunately, Biscay was to live up to its reputation and, in the middle of the crossing, some 170 miles from land, they encountered 45 knot winds. The waves had had 3,000 miles to pick up strength and Malc and Lindy had 30ft-high monsters breaking over their decks.

It was now dark; things always seem bleaker in the darkness. They were both very scared, and not yet used to the way the steel hull reverberated with each breaking wave. *Mr Bean* suddenly seemed very small. Lindy became increasingly seasick and Malc, with every retch from Lindy and every new note from the protesting hull, saw his dream disappearing.

To Guernsey

Malc decided to heave to and ride out the storm. Fortunately, a large container vessel, seeing this small yacht being thrown around, called *Mr Bean* on the VHF and offered to provide a lee. This huge vessel stayed with them through the night. By morning, the wind had subsided and they managed to get under way again. They made it to La Coruña the next day.

Malc said although it had been bad, he still wanted to carry on. He is very strong willed and on occasions he can be overbearing almost to the point of bullying. But, to his eternal credit, he had seen how Lindy had suffered and was quite prepared to leave the decision about whether or not to sail on up to Lindy.

Lindy, as the world was later to witness, is an amazingly brave woman and she rationalised that, although it had been scary, if that was the worst that they would encounter then they shouldn't give up.

Turkey 1992, from left: Ros, Malc, Katie, Lindy, Sophie

To Guernsey

Tristan

Lord we pray the shipwright
has done his job so well,
And that her skippers guide her passage,
all her tales to tell.

She bears the name of Tristan
You kept her namesake sailing,
And now we ask You, Oh Lord,
to save this craft from failing

Give her captains courage
to fetch new ports of call
And sense enough to keep her safe,
her crew, her bill and all.

Calm the seas, dull the wind
make the sun shine bright
And even when the day is done
let the stars give light

Grant us please, one last wish -
That she's a happy ship;
And just for the sight of her,
your heart a beat to skip

***

I have been involved with sailing and boats and most things to do with water since I was a little boy. However, running a business and living in Buckinghamshire didn't allow many opportunities for us to get afloat. Our move to Guernsey changed all that and, in the autumn of 1998, we took delivery of our new Aqua-Star motorboat.

To Guernsey

We named her Tristan after Tristan Jones. On a cold and windy day she was lifted from the trailer by one of the massive cranes on the docks at St Peter Port harbour and gently lowered into her new element.

A small group of family and friends were there for the launch, and little Sophie, who was eight then, read a poem as Tristan was launched. Sophie and I had written the poem one day when we were delayed at the airport trying to get back to the island. It was no literary masterpiece, but it said what we wanted it to say.

Even the big, tough boat builders standing on the quay that day had a tear in their eyes, as little Sophie, buffeted by the wind, spoke strongly in the face of the breeze.

Now I really had the chance for some new challenges and adventures! I was a reasonably experienced yachtsman and had passed my coastal skipper exams. However, I had actually had very little experience of motorboats – especially one weighing 20 tons. It was a steep learning curve, as I grappled with making the boat go where I wanted it to go and learning all the systems on board. I felt a bit like a learner pilot who finds it all right once you are up - it is the landing and the taking off that is the problem. Similarly, manoeuvring a 45ft boat into and out of a packed marina on my own was a bit of a nightmare, but once out at sea I felt that, like Tristan, I was in my element.

Ros too, became more confident about our new boat and we started to talk about possibly taking her to the Mediterranean for the summer. We might even be able to meet up with Malc and Lindy who also planned to still be in the Med before heading out to cross the Atlantic later that year. We had not planned Tristan as a Med boat, but she inspired such confidence that even Ros was excited at the prospect of such a trip.

I managed to secure a mooring for Tristan in Beaucette Marina, which is right in the north-eastern tip of the island. Beaucette was originally a granite quarry and is over 60ft deep in parts. When the quarry was exhausted, the then owner decided to remove a section of the wall that bordered the sea to make a marina. He managed to arrange for the Royal Engineers to visit and blast away the rock for him. The result is one of the most daunting marina entrances in the British Isles.

The narrow fairway leading to the entrance is bordered with rocky outcrops, many of which cover and uncover in the huge nine metre tidal range. The entrance itself is narrow, with high granite outcrops on either side. Because it is exposed to north-easterly winds, waves can break over the entrance, making it impassable. Once inside, though, the visitor is treated to a most beautiful and tranquil marina. In the summer, seals often visit to feast on the large number of grey mullet which make the marina their home. The first time I brought Tristan through the entrance my heart was in my mouth, and even after countless entries and exits, it would still be a guaranteed source of adrenaline for me.

With my episodes now happening so often, I was a little concerned about one occurring while I was alone in the boat. Driving a car was no problem, as the onset was always slow enough to have time to stop or get home. In September 1998 we had a few days away on Tristan with friends, and my worst fears were realised on our way home when I started to feel unwell on the approach to the marina. It wasn't pleasant but I managed to get through the entrance and reverse into the mooring and tie up before I disappeared below to ride out this latest episode. I felt now that if I could do this while having one of my turns, then I could manage most situations in the boat.

We started planning our voyage to the Mediterranean in November. I was obsessive about getting everything right. Having discounted going through the inland waterways of France because Tristan was four inches too high, we knew the only option was the sea route. Another of my dreams had been to cross the Bay of Biscay, and now I might get my chance.

Ros was not at all happy about the prospect of this part of the voyage. It is a notoriously unforgiving and often storm-tossed piece of ocean, where the rollers gather momentum over thousands of miles before arriving in the Bay.

Going straight across would mean one leg of 345 miles from the Brest peninsula to La Coruña. In the middle of this passage we would be 170 miles from land, and out of radio contact. If something went wrong, we would be on our own.

The Biscay crossing would be too much for Ros and the girls and I planned to complete this section of the journey with some sailing buddies of mine. Even so, I tried to plan for every eventuality and to reduce the risks as much as I could.

I had become firm friends with Jon Travers, who then worked for Aqua-Star as an engineer; he had been hugely helpful in teaching me about the boat. Jon was really interested in coming on the journey, and in the end, Ros almost made it a condition of the trip that he had to be there. She knew he would look after the boat and me. Also with us would be Phil Robertson and Peter Davies, sailing mates from England.

We worked out a simple safety plan and the four of us on board knew exactly who would be responsible for what, in case of an emergency. Ros briefed Jon separately about looking after me and he came away with detailed explanations of what drug I was to take when, and what to do when I had a turn.

We set off from Guernsey in June 1999 and had a bumpy crossing to Camaret on the Brest peninsula. A few miles before reaching it we discovered that we had almost lost the dinghy from the davits (the big stainless steel arms that secured the dinghy). The pressure from all the bumpy seas had put such a strain on the davit lifting points that the lifting eye had been pulled right through the hull of the dinghy, along with a great chunk of fibreglass.

There was now a five-inch hole in the bottom of the dinghy. The little boat was swinging in its safety straps and, if these gave way, we would lose the lot. We needed to put something under the hull, attach the davit wire and haul the whole lot up again. I had a shiny new stainless steel jack staff[3], which I had not yet fitted on the bow, and reckoned this might do the trick. We tied a line around the jack staff, passed the davit wire through the hole, and attached it to the staff. As we tightened the wire the dinghy rose neatly back into place.

This lasted about ten minutes. When we hit the first big bump the line holding the staff against the dinghy's hull slackened just long enough for the staff to slip through the loop into the sea. 'Bugger! That was nearly 50 quid's worth,' I said. 'OK', Jon said, 'What we really need is a strong piece of teak. Maybe we can lash it all up until we can get a piece of wood.'

'Hell, I'm sure I have a big piece of teak somewhere,' I replied. I had kept a piece of scrap teak left over from an improvement we had made to the radar arch. I dug it out and within minutes Jon had drilled it, fixed the old lifting eye in place and once again hauled the dinghy back into place. This time it stayed there.

We had planned to get a good meal in Camaret, as this could be our last proper meal for a while. We would be living on snack food for the 34 hours of the Biscay crossing. When we arrived in the French port, it was dark and the wind had whipped up. We couldn't find a space on a jetty. There were lots of mooring buoys, but without a

---

[3] Nautical term for a flag pole, usually small, fitted to the bow of a vessel.

serviceable dinghy, we wouldn't be able to reach the shore. It is customary to go alongside other moored vessels in such circumstances and it is an unwritten law that you should put fenders out to seaward, as well as jetty side, as a welcome to other vessels looking for a berth.

We searched for a boat of comparable length to lie alongside and spotted an immaculate Grand Banks motorboat – perfect! In fact, the Grand Banks was the only boat we could go alongside as the others were tucked in finger berths without room to get two boats in.

We rigged lines and fenders and started the slightly tricky manoeuvre to lie next to the other vessel. The Grand Banks didn't have fenders rigged, but we were not worried, as our large round ones would be more than adequate to protect both boats.

We were perhaps fifteen feet from landing alongside when the English owner appeared from below decks, waving his arms and shouting a torrent of abuse. 'F.... off, f... off. How dare you?! I don't want you alongside my boat. F... off you bastards.'

I was completely taken aback, stunned. I couldn't for the life of me see what his problem was and I couldn't understand his completely unwarranted barrage. I wanted to explain our situation but realised he was in no mood to listen.

I gunned Tristan's engines in order to get some steerage way and to clear his boat. The other chap disappeared below again, not allowing us any opportunity to speak to him. I decided I didn't want to lie alongside someone like him anyway – revolting idiot as he was.

Jon and the others were all for boarding him and trying one or two more traditional maritime methods of persuasion – keelhauling was top of the list. Realising we had other pressing matters to sort out, we picked up a mooring buoy and started to get things ship shape again. We decided to lighten the dinghy by removing the outboard engine and storing it in the engine room. This took about an hour to achieve as the 25 horse power engine was bolted securely to the dinghy and it is very heavy and difficult to manhandle. Instead of a meal ashore, I cooked a Thai chicken curry and we watched a video before getting an early night.

We fuelled up first thing next morning. Jon squeezed every last drop he could into the tanks. We checked the forecast one last time, which gave SW 4-5. Not ideal, not comfortable, but well within Tristan's capabilities and we set off for Spain.

The first couple of hours were OK, a bit bumpy but quite acceptable. Slowly the wind and waves rose until we were in a steady 25-knot breeze. Every wave we hit threw gallons of spray over Tristan and the uncomfortable motion of the boat was unrelenting. We had a conference to ensure everyone was happy to continue and all agreed to press on. The windscreens were continually covered in green water; we could see nothing through them. We saw nothing on the radar either. In fact, it would be another 300 miles before we next saw one single blip on the radar screen. Later, Phil likened the Biscay trip to being in a car wash for 34 hours.

Towards the end of the first day of the crossing I felt the onset of one of my episodes and retired to the aft cabin. I lay there, gritting and grinding my teeth waiting for the waves in my head to subside. As usual, after forty minutes things started to settle down, but I was feeling light headed and sick. I tried to stay in the cabin but there was a strong smell of exhaust fumes. I got up and made my way to the heads (toilet), as I was sure I was going to be sick. I opened the heads door, only to discover that every surface in there was now black. Somehow, exhaust fumes had been sucked into the compartment and the toilet shower, basin and walls were all covered with a fine, black soot. No wonder I had felt sick. I made my way back up to the saloon and explained to the lads. Jon went to investigate and discovered that the basin waste outlet was too near the main exhaust bleed-off. This meant that the air hungry engines were sucking air into the engine room via the aft cabin and heads. Fumes were being sucked back up the basin outlet. To solve the problem Jon put the sink plug in and half filled the basin with water.

I had spent weeks conducting fuel trials as I had to be sure that Tristan's 500-gallon tanks would be adequate for the non-stop passage across the bay. I wanted a safety reserve of 20% and was fairly sure we had this if we crossed at 10 knots. In the end, to be doubly sure, we strapped a 45-gallon fuel drum on the bathing platform and rigged up a pumping system that should work even if the boat was being thrown around in a heavy sea. This reserve supply was almost our undoing, as the massive weight of the drum unseated the hatch into a storage compartment within the bathing platform. The first we knew of this was at 2.30 in the morning when I noticed the aft bilge pump light was on. 'Oh shit,' I said as soon as I saw it. 'What's going on, Jon?'

Jon was sitting on the stairs which go from the saloon up to the aft deck trying to have a cigarette without getting the smoke in the boat and, at the same time, trying not to let the constant deluge of water over the decks come in through the aft door.

'I wouldn't worry, it will probably go out in a minute,' he said. I did worry, and it didn't go out. We ripped up the carpet and boards from the aft cabin to find water lapping at the underside of the boards. There were several tons of water in the bilge. The small bilge pump had burnt out. The large one, which the Managing Director of Aqua-Star had assured me would never be needed, was going hell for leather, pumping huge quantities of water back into the sea. Jon soon found where the water was coming from. There was a two-inch drainpipe from the bathing platform locker into the bilge and there was so much water coming through it that it would have made a fireman proud.

'Take her up to 12 knots,' snapped Jon. 'We need to get her arse out of the water.' He knew immediately that the only way the water was getting in was through the hatch, and that at this slow speed the back of the boat was low in the water. With the heavy sea, waves were constantly breaking over the bathing platform. As soon as I increased speed Tristan's bow dipped a little and her transom[4] rose a few inches. 'It's working,' Jon said. I dashed back into the aft cabin to see the water level dropping at an amazing rate.

Just before we arrived in La Coruña, the sun came out and it shone for the next 10 weeks. Within hours of arriving in La Coruña the boatyard had mended our dinghy. Next day we fuelled up again. We hadn't needed the spare fuel in the drum on the bathing platform, so pumped this in to Tristan's main tanks and donated the drum to the yard; we wouldn't need it again. We did our best to seal up the hatch and continued on the next leg of our journey.

The lads left me in Portugal and after a few days Ros and the girls came out to join me in the sun-baked Algarve port of Lagos. We set sail the next morning and headed for the Balearics, now a mere 700 miles away.

Within two days, we planned to be going through the Straits of Gibraltar. I was excited about this as I'd never been there and also this would mark the point that we entered the Mediterranean. On the morning we made our approach to the Straits, I couldn't believe it, there was thick fog! I was so disappointed – I had been looking forward to seeing that iconic lump of rock and now I was struggling to see further than Tristan's bow.

---

[4] The transom is the back, or back wall, of the hull.

To Guernsey

I suppose we were about 10 miles from Gibraltar when the fog started to thin and then, with a jolt, I saw land on our starboard side. Africa! I was so focussed on our passage to Gibraltar that it hadn't registered how close we were to another continent! The shores of Morocco were only 5 miles away.

We fuelled up in Gibraltar and, as this was all duty free, I made sure the tanks were as full as we could get them. The next day's cruising was one of the most memorable we've ever had. A strong westerly breeze sprang up and by about 10am it was blowing force seven. We were flying.

Tristan is particularly good downwind and we were keeping up a constant 20 knots and now surfing down sizeable waves. Ros was sunbathing on the flybridge and our Guernsey ensign was flapping madly towards the bow. Vessels coming the other way weren't having such a good time and even the largest ships were struggling into the enormously steep waves. The only downside was that my attacks were very frequent now and on several occasions I left Ros in charge while I lay down and rode out each episode. Ros thankfully wasn't too worried, as she knew she could fetch me if our course took us near other ships and she also knew that each attack would be over in less than 50 minutes.

We kept up our surfing for 10 hours and covered more than 200 miles that day. Unlike the passage with the boys across Biscay, we were able to find a marina each night which meant we slept and ate well and the girls didn't get too bored with being at sea all the time. These stops also allowed me to carry out boat maintenance and, boy, there was a lot to do. Tristan was a relatively new boat and naively perhaps, I hadn't realised just how many snagging items I'd have to deal with. I felt quite pressurised as I fixed leaky windows, replaced bilge pumps, traced electrical problems and completed oil changes.

To Guernsey

Six days after Ros and the girls had joined ship, we reached Mallorca. I couldn't believe we had made it - and so quickly. The first part of the voyage from Guernsey to the Algarve, a distance of 1,000 took just 79 hours and, excluding the few days I spent waiting for Ros and the girls to arrive in Portugal, the whole trip, Guernsey to Mallorca took just nine days.

When we arrived in the bay of Pollensa, at the north of the island, there were Malc and Lindy on board Mr Bean, anchored peacefully in the middle of the bay. It all seemed so unreal, to be meeting up again, so far from Guernsey in our own boat.

In all, we clocked up some 5,000 miles on this trip, but with my condition being worse than ever, instead of feeling elated and fulfilled, Ros and I returned exhausted.

Don't get me wrong, I wouldn't have missed that trip for anything and I don't regret doing it. We had so many experiences and learnt so much, but this all came at a bit of a price.

The crunch came when on top of having two, sometimes three, episodes a day, I ended up in hospital with a completely unrelated problem.

We were at anchor one night in Fornells Bay in Menorca. I was head down in a locker, fiddling with the water maker when my nose started to bleed. Straight away I knew this was not an ordinary bleed. There was a constant flow of blood, like a tap turned partly on. Nothing I did would stop the flow. When I tried squeezing my nose it just flowed backwards and came out of my mouth. I was certain that I had burst an artery.

Thank heavens our good friends Wendy and Phil Robertson were staying with us. Phil, who had helped with the Biscay trip, was now over for a week with his family. I said to Phil, as calmly as possible: 'Phil you'd better get me to hospital quickly – I think this is serious.'

To Guernsey

Wendy volunteered to stay and look after the children while Phil, Ros and I got into Tristan's tender for the short trip to land. By this time I had half a kitchen roll scrunched up to my nose and I was having trouble breathing, there was so much blood.

Phil was cruising along like it was a Sunday afternoon jaunt down the Thames. 'Crikey, Phil, get a move on, I'm bleeding to death here!' I managed to splutter and Phil threw the throttle open wide. In seconds we were skimming over the sea and salty spray was now mixing with the blood dripping from my hand clasping the paper towel to my nose.

Phil slightly misjudged our landing and we rammed the sea wall so hard that we bounced straight back. 'I meant to do that,' he quipped, before correcting his error and jumping on to the quay. We had to walk through a busy restaurant to get to the road and everyone was staring at us. Ros approached a waiter to ask how to get to a doctor but the chap just stared at me, and the huge bundle of bloody paper in front of my face.

At this point Ros lost it. 'Look here, you cretin, my husband is bleeding to death – don't just gawp, help us!' He pointed towards a small line of taxis and amazingly we managed to find one willing to take this motley, bloody collection of sailors to Mahon – a good half-hour's drive away.

By the time I managed to see a doctor the bleeding had stopped and the doctor sent me away without doing anything.

We went back to the boat, but the next morning, as soon as I got up, the bleeding started again. I was still bleeding when we arrived at the hospital and I was sent straight to an ear nose and throat specialist. It wasn't helpful that this chap kept telling me how serious it was 'Very 'portant, very 'portant, muy difficile, difficult, difficult,' he kept repeating as he worked.

To Guernsey

Ros was made to wait in the adjoining room, but she could hear everything that was going on. The doctor reached for this really long probe thing and made as if he was going to put it up my nose.

'Whoa there,' I said. 'I have come here to have my nose fixed, not brain surgery.' The doctor said, 'this hurtin' a bit – no worry', and rammed the instrument up my nose. Immediately, he and I were both covered in blood. The doctor turned on some sort of suction tube that did at least stop the pool on the floor growing any more. Instead, the blood was cunningly diverted to a collection bottle situated in the next room - where Ros was waiting.

Now, what with the sounds coming from the next room and the fast-filling bottle, Ros was nearly beside herself with worry.

I then had two *tampanellas* (tampons) rammed up my nose and was advised to lie down for a week. I did as advised and lay on my back, bored to tears. This wasn't much fun for everyone else, either.

This episode had really ruined Phil and Wendy's holiday as it meant we were all stuck in harbour in Mahon for the week. It really hit home with Ros when Katie was talking to her about being worried that the nose problem was somehow connected to MS and she started to weep and asked, 'Is Daddy going to die?'

This was all too much for Ros; she thought we had enough challenges already and didn't need the added excitement of adventuring. At the end of the week I returned to the doctor, successfully had the tampons removed, and soon after we made our way back to Guernsey.

On our way back we said goodbye to Malc and Lindy, they sailed off to head out of the Med too, but they were then heading south to the Azores to start their Atlantic crossing. We headed north, back towards colder climates.

Chapter four - Background to a world record

"He that will not sail until all dangers are over must never put to sea."
Thomas Fuller

In 2000, Guernsey's Fitness Factory rowing team, led by local sporting hero Colin Fallaize, rowed non-stop from Guernsey to the Millennium Dome in London to provide funds for the Multiple Sclerosis Society. Without knowing I had the disease, they asked me if I could help by using my boat as a guard boat, but unfortunately I was already committed during that time. The main sponsor, Barings, helped organise the row and assisted with the fundraising.

In 2002 I became involved with the attempt to row non-stop from Guernsey to Amsterdam and agreed to use my boat as a guard boat. Once again, Barings sponsored the attempt and all proceeds went to the MS Society. It failed, as bad weather forced us to take shelter in Blankenberg, Belgium. However, the team went on with the row once the weather had cleared and they raised about £18,000 for the Society.

It was also in this year that the frequency of my attacks lessened and then completely stopped. I think I could safely say I was in remission. In all, I had been having the episodes for nearly seven years - I was so relieved not to be suffering them anymore.

At the end of the Amsterdam row Colin said, 'Never again!' but within a few days there was discussion about the next project. Also there were rumours about a team from Jersey planning to have a go at the world record London-to-Paris row. This had been attempted twice before and the Ditton Skiffers, a team led by the explorer and rower Jock Wishart, then held the record. The Jersey team blew the Skiffers' record apart and set a new time of

90 hours, 33 minutes and 33 seconds. This was a fantastic achievement especially considering the team encountered very difficult conditions in the Channel and even took shelter in Le Havre for a few hours. Although the old record had been broken by a large margin the Jersey team felt, with better weather, it could be lowered again.

Colin Fallaize's involvement with the MS Society started in the 1980s. He was working as a fitness instructor at Guernsey's sports centre, Beau Sejour. One day he was rushing to get to work and there was a queue of people going very slowly down the stairs. Colin remembers being impatient and thinking – 'What the hell is the hold up – get a move on'. Having pushed to the front he was confronted with an MS sufferer struggling to get down the stairs. He felt terrible and vowed never to be so impatient, to have more understanding and, crucially, to do something to help people who have MS.

It was only a couple of months after this that a good friend of Colin's, someone he had been at school with and worked alongside at Beau Sejour, contracted the disease. Steve Le Poidevin had been about as active as a person can be and now he had been struck with this terrible illness. Steve had primary progressive MS that had progressed fairly quickly[5]. Colin's resolve to help battle MS strengthened.

Erik Selvidge was a founder member of the local MS Society branch and had been chairman for many years. Erik's wife has MS and, as he wanted to spend more time with her, he decided to give up the reins of chairmanship he had held so ably for many years. Colin was a natural successor and, even with all his other responsibilities, he didn't hesitate in agreeing to become the new chairman.

Liz Hendry had been an active member of the MS Society and committee member for a number of years.

---

[5] Steve Le Poidevin sadly passed away in January 2012.

Liz's involvement started when a friend of hers, Josephine Ozanne, who was a physiotherapist, asked her if she could provide some regular help to a sufferer in the area. Liz willingly agreed and her involvement with the society blossomed from there. Strangely, Josephine, then contracted the disease herself.

When Erik stepped down as chairman, Liz encouraged her accountant husband Ron to take on the task of treasurer. Ron is a Scottish whirlwind, but the most organised whirlwind you could meet. This new committee set about reviewing the services available to people with MS in the Bailiwick of Guernsey and came to the conclusion that, in line with the UK, an MS nurse could help sufferers substantially.

In the UK more than 100 MS nurses had been appointed and their main task was to coordinate services available to MS sufferers. Guernsey does not have a comprehensive health service and relies quite heavily on agreements with the UK health service to provide treatments not available in the island. For instance, until 1997 the island did not have an MRI machine, so scans had to be carried out in Southampton.

Generally the system works quite well, but it falls down where long-term care and specialist knowledge are needed. The island also did not have a neurologist or anyone with specific training and understanding about MS. This means people who develop MS in Guernsey will be diagnosed in the UK and then, when they get home, there will be no sophisticated support for them or their families. Help for the family is crucial at that stage and the need for sympathetic and professional management of the early days is, quite simply, essential.

The next target, then, for our intrepid MS Society committee was to find the money to finance a specialist nurse. In the UK the society would typically fund a nurse for three years and, when his or her worth had been established, the local health service was persuaded to fund the position permanently.

The committee realised that three years' costs would be about £90,000. Annually, the branch raised an average of £30,000, but most of this was already needed to fund essential expenditure on equipment and improvements. However, there was a general feeling among committee members that islanders would be very supportive of the MS nurse project and that with a good push perhaps they could raise this sum within three years.

Colin, known for his quotes, had said about the Amsterdam row: 'MS gives us the reason – fitness gives us the chance.' This maxim seemed to hold good still and Colin's mind was made up - another big rowing project was needed.

Chapter five – The devil is in the detail

"Success in any endeavour requires single-minded attention to detail and total concentration."
Willie Sutton (one of the most ingenious bank robbers of all time)

Colin had mentioned the London to Paris row to me a few times and we had even discussed building a high-tech boat for the event.

Colin received a Channel Islands sporting hero award in 2002 and Pete Goss, the celebrated yachtsman and challenge organiser, came to the island to present it. Colin and I had previously met Pete at a talk he gave in Guernsey. It seemed natural, then, to discuss the project with him. He was enthusiastic about building a carbon fibre rowing boat and even perhaps introducing a radical catamaran design.

In November 2003, Colin said: 'Well, I think we should have a crack at it – I reckon May might be a good time.'

'OK,' I said, 'That gives us 18 months to get ready, which should be enough time.' 'No,' Colin said, 'I mean May 2004, not 2005 – anyway, I reckon we were a bit over-prepared last time.'

I remember going home and having a quick look at the route. The row would be almost 480 miles. It would be incredibly difficult to go that far on flat water, let alone having to cope with wind and waves. We would have to negotiate two major rivers and the busiest shipping lanes in the world. We would need a mountain of equipment and the red tape would be hideous. I really was not sure this was actually do-able.

Barings, who had helped so magnificently with past events, had said that while they would continue to support the MS Society, the Amsterdam row would be the last

83

such event they would be involved in. Knowing this, Colin asked whether I would consider helping with the organisation. We had a short discussion about what was really quite a momentous decision. Colin, like most good leaders and believers in teamwork, is not restrained by his own limitations but has enormous belief in the abilities of others. He will take on a task knowing he hasn't a chance of doing it himself, but he knows how to find and inspire people who can.

We knew we wouldn't have Barings' organisational abilities with us on this one, but we felt, when it came to fundraising, it might actually help if people knew the rowing team were doing everything themselves. I agreed to head the organising committee and set about finding volunteers and mapping out the committee's objectives.

I knew I needed to find a team with diverse skills, who all had one thing in common. Throughout my career I had been very wary of committees. I hated the slow, lumbering process and the prospect of decisions born through soft compromises and weak leadership. I needed a team of people who were self-starters: doers with brains. It is perhaps no coincidence that the committee ended up being almost exclusively composed of successful entrepreneurs. It is worth recording who these people were, because every one of the rowers will acknowledge that at least a part of their world record was earned by these folks.

Ron Hendry – Treasurer of the local MS branch, then an 'almost retired' accountant who achieved more in a morning's work than most people do in a week. Ron was most definitely the backbone of the committee. If the devil is in the detail then Ron was to be our chief exorcist.

Colin Fallaize – Row team leader and owner of the Fitness Factory gym in Guernsey. Colin would be responsible for all things to do with the rowers and rowing. His main tasks were team selection, training and communication with rowers. Colin is also the face of the Guernsey rowers and most media attention would revolve around him. He is very well known in the Channel Islands as a sportsman with exceptional skills and as an extraordinarily gifted coach.

John Neale – John is a retired journalist and was always swift to write and edit media releases and other such material. His knowledge of the local media scene was invaluable. John is also into all things nautical and this watery challenge was enough to tempt him to help us with his undoubted literary skills.

Roger Martel – Roger was our wild card, but that card was definitely from the suit of hearts. His career has been wide ranging: he has been a fisherman, a fireman and a builder. Roger now has his own very successful building and property development company. He is a keen sailor and as well as a very hairy *Melges* racing yacht he owned a huge 54-foot Sunseeker Predator motorboat. Roger stepped in at 48 hours' notice on the Amsterdam row when one of the arranged guard boats blew an engine. Even though his boat took a bit of a battering on the last rowing challenge, Roger had no hesitation in offering it and his own services for the next challenge. He is an ideas man and many of his ideas are pretty wild, but often he sees a way of doing something that can only be described as random lateral thinking. Most of all, Roger is enthusiastic and strains to be let loose to get on with things.

David Read – David is our gentleman businessman. He had a commercial estate agency business in the U.K. and is another 'almost retired' committee member. He has solid ideas that he puts forward in an eloquent and diplomatic manner. Although task-orientated and focused he always has time for the social graces. David was also to join the guard boat crew aboard Roger Martel's boat *Lecca Lecca*. While often acting as a calming influence, at the same time he was responsible for some of the boldest steps the committee was to take.

John Tostevin – I didn't know John, but he came highly recommended by other team members. He too is an extremely successful businessman, yet on first acquaintance he was quiet and reserved. During our early meetings he sat silently, taking it all in. As time went on he grew in stature and confidence and it became clear that he was a chap determined to succeed. If John volunteers to do something it is as good as done. He also has a magical sense of humour – completely wicked, very quick and often based on the observation of others.

David Farrimond - A Bolton Wanderers supporter and Lancashire through and through, David is another of our 'almost retired' accountants. I knew when I asked him that he was already busy with other charitable work and he had also recently flung himself, full tilt, into a French degree course. But, I also knew if I could stir up a bit of interest, his communication and organisational skills would be very useful to the team.

David agreed to join the committee and took on a number of tasks including being our anchorman and communicator in Guernsey. It would have been David's unenviable task to coordinate with the authorities, relatives and press had any disaster happened. We realised the organisers had a serious responsibility here and that poor organisation at such a time would be both inexcusable and cruel.

The devil is in the detail

The Cullingtons - Geoff Cullington had been a key member of the Amsterdam row team and was the main navigator for that event. He had been due to use his boat, an Aqua-Star 38, as lead guard boat, but it blew an engine just a couple of days before the event was due to start. Roger Martel came forward at the last moment and offered his Sunseeker for the role and Geoff and his son Tony joined the crew of *Lecca Lecca* for the trip to Holland.

Since the Amsterdam row, Geoff had retired and moved from Guernsey to Carteret in France. I tried to recruit his services with his newly repaired boat *Symphony* but he was already committed to a round-Britain cruise. However, he generously offered his time to help sort out various permissions needed from the French and British authorities and he offered to assist with the passage planning for the event. Geoff's passage planning has actually won awards and I was really delighted to be able to call on his services.

As the project progressed, Geoff and his wife, Joan, became increasingly involved in the arrangements and spent many days dashing around various parts of France and England, visiting a selection of maritime and river authorities.

It became obvious that we would need a shore-based support team in England and in France and the Cullingtons were again quick to come forward to provide this support. 'What about your cruise?' I asked Geoff. 'Oh don't worry about that. I have already briefed the other boat on our cruise – you just give us 48 hours' notice and we will dash back to London for the start and then nip over to France to do the French shore crew bit.'

The entire Cullington family are talented linguists and their fluent French was immensely helpful.

The devil is in the detail

The rowers - Colin Fallaize was to be responsible for all things to do with the rowing team, from deciding how big it should be, to selection, training and motivation. The Jersey record had been set with 21 rowers and Colin was determined to break their time using a smaller team. He settled on 16 rowers rowing five at a time. If the Guernsey team did manage to break the record with fewer rowers it meant any successive challenge would have to use the same number or fewer.

This configuration would mean each rower would row for an hour then have an hour off. Each rower would get a five-hour break at least once during the challenge. Many people questioned this, believing longer rest periods would be needed over the four days. The rowers had proved on earlier challenges that the system is effective and, while there is no doubt that rowers do not really get much quality sleep, they seem to be able to remain at a constant state of readiness for a long period.

No one knew, however, whether it was workable over such a long time. We knew other teams had suffered through some individuals getting to the point where they refused to row their shift.

Colin insisted he knew each of his team members intimately and was absolutely confident he knew the strengths and weaknesses of each individual. He was sure that no one would let the team down. I had seen this team spirit in action during the Amsterdam row. Sam de Kooker, for instance, had suffered terribly from seasickness almost from the moment we had left Guernsey. His father, Adek, was also one of the rowers and every hour he would just say 'It's time, son,' and Sam would remove his head from the bucket he had spent the last hour staring into, don his lifejacket and get into the rowing boat for another hour's work.

Mark Windsor had used the last fifteen minutes of each rest hour trying to stick plasters on the flesh of his fingers that had been rubbed raw by the friction from the oars and which were stinging with the constant soaking from sea water. Others suffered terrible cramps and their teammates gave up their rest periods in order to massage their friends' cramped muscles and provide moral support. One team member rubbed his scrotum raw and was in so much pain it was almost impossible for him to walk.

The team would be split into two, with one half based on Tristan and the other on Lecca Lecca. In addition to the 16, Colin decided he should select another rower to act as a reserve, just in case any of the team was ill or unable to complete the challenge for any other reason. Of the eight rowers on board each guard boat, there would always be three resting and five either on their hour row or on their hour break.

At this point, I should try to convey some sense of just how difficult this row was going to be. If you are a person of average height, weight and fitness, but someone not used to rowing, you might be able to keep up the stroke rate and distance per stroke needed for perhaps, for five minutes. In those five minutes your heart rate will have increased to your physical maximum and you will be gasping for breath. Even regular users of rowing machines seldom row for as long as an hour. Our rowers were going to row for an hour, every other hour, for over three days, and they would be rowing hard.

Aside from the sheer physical strength and mental stamina required, they would need to be skilled and brave enough to cope with rowing at sea and at night, across one of the busiest shipping lanes in the world. This would be a monumental trial of strength and determination. Rowing is mighty good exercise, but rowing like this would be at the extreme end of extreme.

Training began in December and because of the generally poor weather it was almost exclusively on land.

The devil is in the detail

Each team member spent many hours each week on rowing machines either within group training or as individuals. Colin organised early morning runs along the cliff paths and kept tabs on the progress of each member. The lads were desperate to get back on the water, as while the rowing machine is an excellent alternative, it will never provide training needed to row as a part of a team.

Chapter six - The plan

"The sea has been much maligned. To find one's way to lands already discovered is a good thing, and the Spray made the discovery that even the worst sea is not so terrible to a well-appointed ship."
Joshua Slocum

Within a few days of assembling the team, I set about preparing an outline plan for presentation to the committee. This was fleshed out during our first meeting and pretty soon we developed a project checklist that was to become the reference document for every part of the project. The team met every two weeks and such was the commitment to the plan that we seldom experienced any significant slippage in achieving the agreed tasks.

This initial planning, however, did little to improve my confidence in our overall chances of succeeding and it was increasingly obvious that the opportunities for failure were massive.

The Boats

Early on we realised we could afford neither the time nor the money to build a new rowing boat. The one we had used for the last challenge was not now set up for such a thing, but there was a sister boat owned by local company Geomarine which, if they could be persuaded to let us use it, might be set up for the row. The firm had supported the MS Society with past projects and again readily agreed to lend the team Geomarine Challenger. Once Colin got his hands on it, he realised that it too actually needed a lot of work to set it up and make it strong enough for the challenge ahead. Alas, we hadn't much of a budget for refurbishment.

Colin had the idea of asking some of the inmates in Guernsey's prison to help. He worked there for a number of hours each week, supervising fitness sessions. Members of the prison staff were looking for worthwhile community projects that could involve prisoners, and Colin's idea seemed tailor-made.

Eric Selvidge's son worked there and with his assistance it was arranged to deliver Geomarine Challenger to the jail. The boat was given over to the care of three inmates who had volunteered for the work. Under the guidance of prison officer Selvidge, they completely stripped the boat down and rebuilt it. Before starting work they produced detailed technical drawings and specifications to which the boat was to be rebuilt. All the seams were re-taped and epoxied and, once the inmates had built a dust-proof plastic tent, she was repainted to an incredible standard. The three young lads completed the most remarkable refurbishment and at the handing back ceremony they were justly proud of their achievement.

In addition to a rowing boat, we knew we would need a big rigid inflatable boat (Rib) and three support boats to house the eleven off-duty crew members, the two off-duty Rib crew, TV crew, photographer, doctor and of course the 12 people needed to crew the support boats themselves. In all, there would be 35 people on the water.

Roger Martell came forward with his 54-foot Sunseeker and Buz White didn't have to have his arm twisted too much before he too volunteered to support us with his fast sea charter boat, Access Challenger. Obviously I would use Tristan, so now we just had to lay hands on a suitable Rib.

We tried all the leads we could think of to find one. Actually, we had lots of offers, but most of the boats were too small, with insufficient range. What we needed was a whopping great 10-metre job with an inboard diesel engine. Such a craft would make the entire journey under its own steam, rather than having to be towed when not being used at changeover times. Being the same length as the rowing boat, a ten-metre one would pitch in a similar manner to the rowing boat, which would make changeovers simpler and safer. Trouble was, there was only one like this in Guernsey.

The boat in question was brand new, built to a fantastic standard by a local boat yard and worth a fortune. On my way to see Mark Nightingale, manager of the yard, I kept saying to myself, 'nothing ventured, nothing gained' and 'if you don't ask you don't get', but nothing I could say to myself stopped me from feeling very awkward about my plan to ask to use this very special boat. Mark listened to my tale of woe and didn't say anything until I had laid the whole plan out in front of him.

'Well,' he began, 'We are actually trying to sell the boat. We have spent a lot of time and money building it – it really is time we converted all that investment back into cash.'

I thought this was going to be the end of it, but he went on: 'But, if we don't sell it by, say, a month before you are due to go, then yes, you lot can borrow it, but you'd better bring it back in one piece!'

We were a little over three months away from going and every day from then on I dreaded the phone call to say they had sold the Rib. We didn't stop looking for alternatives and did have a smaller one lined up, just in case, but we all knew how important the Boatworks Rib was to us. However, the safety group identified a weakness, in that the big Rib had only one engine. If that were to develop a problem we wouldn't have a back-up. The group recommended that we carry loads of spares for the engine, and in addition, we should try to get a complete back-up Rib. We knew that the Jersey team had run into problems when they burst one of the tubes of theirs, and we had to make sure that didn't happen to us. We couldn't see any other option but to take a complete back-up boat with us. Lecca Lecca has quite a large garage extending under her aft deck and we reckoned that we could get a five-or six-metre inflatable boat, rolled up, plus outboard, in there, which, if we were desperate, could substitute for the big Rib.

Again, we asked everyone we knew and trawled around the boat yards but couldn't find anything remotely adequate. I was so sure that we had to have this equipment that I even started to consider buying a new boat with the idea of selling it 'as new' after the event. Then we decided to put an appeal to the media and this grabbed their attention. We had great coverage and our plea for help was aired non-stop by the local radio.

The next day, I received a call from a company called Comprop to say they had a brand new inflatable and a four-stroke engine that we could borrow. The whole package fitted sweetly into Lecca Lecca's garage and yet another little challenge had been conquered. We didn't stop sweating over the Rib, though, and I have to admit to having terribly uncharitable thoughts about every prospective buyer we heard about.

In early May, Mark Nightingale called and at last put me at ease about the Rib. 'If a buyer turns up now we will explain about the challenge and tell them we have committed to you. The Rib is yours for the challenge.'

Gary Seabrook, one of the four Rib drivers, had been keeping in regular contact, as he was enthusiastic about the challenge and eager to get his hands on the Rib. As soon as he heard the news he was down at the Rib checking everything over and giving 'Boatworks+' a good scrub and tidy.

Gary is very mechanically minded and set about putting together a list of spares and equipment needed and checking over the major systems. He also rigged a protective layer of carpet on the starboard sponson[6] so that we didn't damage the Rib and there was no chance of

---

[6] Traditionally a sponson is part of a boat which extends from the side of a boat to aid stability. In the case of a Rib these are often inflatable tubes.

bursting the sponson, as the Jersey crew had. I felt very confident in our Rib drivers and Gary in particular took a leading role in getting it ready for sea. He knew how important this bit of kit was and treated it as if it was his own.

We split the rowing team in half: eight would be based on Tristan and eight on Lecca Lecca. Both boats would have a crew of four, two on duty at a time, working four-hour shifts. Buz's boat would be home to the two off-duty Rib drivers and they too would work in four-hour shifts. Access Challenger would also provide sleeping space for Liam and Warren, the camera crew, although they were expected to move from boat to boat during the challenge.

Safety
Safety was to be our first and most important objective and a sub-committee with representatives from the rowers and guard boat crews was formed to carry out a risk assessment of all parts of the row. The committee was tasked with identifying possible hazards and ways of minimising significant risks. Its work shaped all the safety training and resulted in a number of procedures being formulated, which not only increased safety but also saved time.

Interestingly, when we contacted the Port of London Authority to obtain advice and request permissions for the event, the first thing they asked for was our risk assessment.

The committee consisted of the skippers of each guard boat, a representative from the rowers and one from the Rib crew. Their brief was to devise a risk management strategy. Within this they would carry out risk assessments for all parts of the row and identify procedures, training and equipment needed to fulfil the safety plan.

The Plan

I had had quite a bit of experience with safety planning in my own business and it is, frankly, not usually an exciting pastime. It requires great attention to detail and discipline, as the whole point is not to miss anything that might cause a problem. The entire process can be laborious and often you are planning for events which will not happen.

Strangely, though, as well as discipline, hard work and thoroughness, you also need imagination. Many of the disasters in the world have been at least partly attributed to a lack of imagination on the part of planners and designers. So, we held these slightly surreal meetings where we laboured through a mass of known possible dangers interspersed with incredible flights of fancy, while we tried to imagine everything that might go wrong. Once we had produced this massive list of dangers, we had to sort them into how likely each was and how damaging it might be. From there, we went on to find ways of eliminating or reducing the risks.

I was a bit disappointed to hear that one or two members of the team had been mocking this safety planning, as they believed it was unnecessary and 'over the top'.

Guernsey folk consider themselves good, safe seafarers and for the most part I would agree with them. There are a few, however, who see going to sea as some sort of macho challenge - even wearing lifejackets is seen by some as a bit sissy. Consequently, it is not as rare as it should be for us to lose fishermen and leisure boat crews to the sea.

There had actually been some sceptics within the safety committee itself, but with each successive meeting, the understanding of the importance of, and interest in, the work we were doing grew.

Having recently read Sir Ernest Shackleton's book about his last expedition, it struck me that even for such a bold adventurer the safety of his team was paramount.

The Plan

Shackleton is remembered as the hero who got everyone back from a series of desperate situations. Significantly, the fact that he failed in his quest to cross the South Polar continent seems almost irrelevant.

There were a number of notable observations and decisions that came out of the planning. While we had always planned to have people with first aid training on each guard boat, we had not intended to have a doctor with us.

The decision to find one wasn't actually just taken on safety grounds. The safety group had discussed what action should be taken if somebody was injured during the row. Obviously the planned actions depended somewhat on where the team was when the injury occurred. It was the possibility of injury at sea that exercised our minds the most.

We realised that a doctor would be able to give a level of immediate care that no first-aider could offer. He or she could perform procedures such as giving injections and performing minor surgery. It also became clear to us that there were many types of injury that, if they occurred during the sea part of the journey, would probably bring the challenge to a halt. Without a doctor on board we would have to err very much on the side of caution and this might mean we would stop the attempt when actually the injury was not that serious.

We felt we wanted a doctor to be pivotal in any decision to stop the row on medical grounds. Within 24 hours of the safety group's decision, Dr Ian Gee had been recruited.

The safety team produced an enormous list of equipment needed and the list was then subdivided into guard boats. While going through it, Buz White said: 'We need scraps of ply, screws and marine glue in case the rowing boat is damaged.'

I was aware that the Jersey team had developed a leak in their boat, but ours was a completely different design and was fitted with self-bailers. I said: 'I can't see that we will need them, but let's take them as they won't take up much room.'

Buz pointed out that we actually already had loads of plywood available as we could use the tops of his lockers if necessary. Without this precaution, and Buz's imagination, the team might not have completed the row.

The safety committee also caused our budget a bit of strain as it identified a number of bits of kit that we would have to buy and that would not be available to borrow from anybody. Among these were emergency lights for life jackets at about £15 each. This doesn't sound much but to kit out the whole team we would need thirty-five of them. I suggested that perhaps we fit them only to the rowers' lifejackets. Roger Martel said: 'We'll leave it to you then, Rob, to explain to the wife of a guard boat crew member why her husband couldn't be found after he fell overboard at night.' That sealed it – 35 lights it was.

While the focus of the safety group was obviously on our project and the safety of our team members, it became apparent that our flotilla of vessels had a duty of care to others and this included other vessels during the event. The group therefore even devised plans and procedures to be followed if we received calls to assist other vessels in distress.

This meant that in the event that we received such a call, there would be no debate and no confusion. It meant that we could react to such events without endangering our own team and it also meant we identified a number of scenarios where, while one of our guard boats might provide assistance, that might not necessarily mean the challenge would be halted or even slowed.

Another significant point to come out of the safety group's work was the need for someone within the team to have overall control of the project during the challenge. When the Amsterdam row had to be halted due to weather conditions, the experienced seafarers in the team were fortunately of one opinion and all agreed the boats should seek shelter.

Looking back on this, it was clear that if the conditions had been more marginal there might not have been such agreement. On that row, while Colin was clearly the leader of the rowers, there was not an agreed decision-maker with regard to the safety and operation of the guard boat team during the challenge.

Our research on previous attempts and lessons learnt from rather more famous feats of human endeavour were essential here. Previous attempts at the London-to-Paris record had perhaps been marked by confused leadership and poor planning. Several of the previous attempts employed the services of 'cross-channel pilots'. As far as I know there is no such thing officially, but I think the term refers generally to skippers of small, commercially registered vessels that have been used as guard boats by cross-channel swimmers.

Problems came with some of the previous rows when these 'pilots' insisted on overall control while at sea. Many of the rowers would be in awe of them and only too happy to agree to it. This would have been fine if the pilots had been involved in the planning, had an appreciation of a safety plan and had been involved in putting together an integrated passage plan. It would also have been okay if the skippers of the other guard boats had agreed that the pilot was in charge.

To illustrate this point, on previous attempts there had been arguments about the order in which guard boats should fuel up, about taking shelter and even about the order in which boats should enter locks.

The pilot involved with the Jersey team led the team in to Le Havre harbour to rest because they were too early for the tide. Then, as a tidal sill trapped them in the harbour, they missed the start of the flood tide that should have pushed them up the Seine.

Technically, each skipper is ultimately in charge and legally responsible for his own vessel and crew. We needed each of the guard boat skippers and indeed the whole team to agree that there would be one overall decision maker. I felt that this would only be workable if everyone had confidence in the agreed decision-making process and the person vested with this responsibility. As all the guard boat skippers were involved in safety planning, we were halfway there already. We planned a safety briefing and information evening as the start of the safety training process and agreed that we would cover the point of decision maker at the meeting.

It was duly agreed that all operation and safety decisions during the challenge would be made following consultation with Colin and the skippers and all agreed that the final decision on these matters would rest with me. While this was a heavy responsibility, I gained comfort from the fact that I had confidence in my fellow skippers and from the tremendous work the safety group had already achieved.

Passage Planning, Pilotage and Permissions.

Geoff Cullington did some research on the permissions needed from the French authorities and I made some similar checks for the Thames and English Channel waters.

Geoff discovered that there are five sections of the Seine, controlled by three authorities – two based in Rouen and one in Paris. In addition, we had to obtain permissions from the Admiral of Cherbourg to cross the French part of the Channel. Geoff also visited the French coastguard authorities at Cap Gris Nez and Jerbourg.

The Plan

Each of the French authorities wanted slightly different information and we ended up sending details of the structure and aims of the project, together with copies of the insurance for each boat, the event insurance, disclaimers leaving the French authorities blameless for any disaster or failure and details of the qualifications of the guard boat crews. Also, each of the helms of the boats had to possess European inland waterways qualifications. This last requirement led to 12 of our crew taking and passing the required course and examination.

On the English side, I found that permissions from the two Port of London (PLA) authority districts could be obtained from one contact and I was put in touch with Ray Blair, deputy Harbour Master of the upper section. The Port of London requirements were quite stringent and not a little taxing, but Ray made things easier by being very clear and precise and by always responding quickly to our questions. We also contacted the Dover Coastguard regarding the section of the row that was to go through British maritime waters.

The Port of London authority required us to have undertaken a full risk assessment for the event and to arrange £5 million pounds' event insurance. We had already planned to do a risk assessment so that was not a problem, but organising the insurance was really difficult. Ron Hendry has considerable experience of the world of insurance, but even he struggled to find a company interested in quoting. Having worked for about a month on the problem, Ron eventually managed to arrange cover, albeit at an alarming price.

Reading through the PLA bylaws, I found that no advertising was allowed on the river. As we were frantically trying to sell advertising space on the rowboat, this requirement came as a bit of a shock. We discussed the problem with the PLA and pointed out that this was for a good cause. They suggested we send a graphic of what we expected the rowboat to look like and they would study it to see if they could allow us to retain the sponsors' logos. Having sent our illustration, a compromise was reached and we agreed there would be no advertising on the guard boats while in the Thames. We also agreed to make the logos on the rowing boat a bit smaller.

Negotiations with the French authorities had a very different timbre and varied from district to district. One common thing was the pride each of the officials had in their various sections. The Seine above Rouen has six locks which normally worked within certain hours. We had to be sure that the lock keepers would open them in the middle of the night and, if possible, have them ready and waiting for us to enter on arrival. If we had to wait for a lock cycle it could mean adding 20 or 30 minutes to our time. All the districts agreed to open the locks on request and further agreed that there would be no charge for openings out of normal hours.

We wrote to all the various officials, requesting written permission and they started to arrive in dribs and drabs. Then we received an unexpected reply from the Admiral of Cherbourg, denying us permission to cross the French shipping lanes.

This was a bombshell.

His reply came so late that it did not give us time to appeal through the requisite channels. Perhaps I am a bit cynical, but I even imagined he had delayed his reply to ensure we could not appeal. His reasoning was that the shipping lanes were very hazardous, meant only for commercial shipping and that the risk of collision was too great to allow us to proceed.

He invited us to alter our project either to take a route around the western end of the traffic separation scheme or to make this a coastal passage. To go around the western end of the scheme would add about 15 miles or three hours to our journey. The coastal passage idea was a complete non-starter.

I was very unhappy with this decision, as I believed it to have dismissed our project out of hand and, worse, to have actually increased the danger to our team, not reduced it. If we crossed the shipping lanes under the watchful eye of the English and French radars and with notices to shipping advising of our flotilla, then the risk of collision would be much less than if we made a crossing over the unregulated part of the channel.

Within the shipping lanes, we could be confident about the direction in which each vessel was travelling. Outside the lanes and particularly at the western end, vessels can enter and leave the scheme at any angle.

All the guard boats possessed good quality radar and navigation systems and the skippers and crews were very experienced and well qualified. In fact, two of the skippers held commercial skippers' tickets and the other has something like 50,000 sea miles under his belt. Thousands of small sailing vessels cross the shipping lanes each year, many of them going slower than our rowing boat and many of them are less manoeuvrable than the rowing boat. Why then did we need special permission?

I also feel strongly that the sea is there for everyone to use and that just because a vessel is delivering fridges to Holland, that shouldn't mean that it necessarily has priority. The Admiral's decision may have absolved him of any blame if we did have a collision, but to me it did seem a weak and not particularly well considered response to a reasonable request.

The response from the Dover coastguard was, in my opinion, far more professional. They made it clear that while they do not support what they call 'unorthodox crossings' they will give advice to make them as safe as possible and also pointed out that they do not have the power to stop such crossings. Their view is that if someone is determined to make a crossing they would far rather know about it so that they can warn other shipping. They did, however, confirm that the French admiral did have the power to stop our flotilla and that they recommended we comply with his requirements.

I couldn't give up on this problem and arranged to see Rob Barton, Guernsey's harbourmaster, to see if he had any ideas. Rob is a very experienced mariner and is hugely respected in the island for his professional abilities. I had intended to make contact with him anyway to apprise him of the project.

Our PR plan included ensuring we had the backing of the harbourmaster's office. Rob was always the first figure of authority to be approached in Guernsey (particularly by the media) for his views on any maritime issue. We spread a chart of the English Channel on his desk and I explained our intended route and the problem posed by the French Admiral.

Almost immediately, Rob pointed out a significant fact that, while it had been staring me in the face, I had just not seen. The boundary between British and French waters did not actually go down the middle of the two lanes of the separation scheme and in fact most of the scheme is actually within British waters. Technically we could cross the separation scheme, albeit a little further to the west than originally planned, and the French could not stop us. However, Rob agreed that if we didn't keep to the spirit of the French requirements we might not receive the co-operation we so desperately needed.

We continued to discuss this problem at length in committee and tried to come up with ways of not having to comply or of perhaps simply disregarding the French authorities. Some of the committee members reckoned we shouldn't have asked in the first place, but in the end the group agreed we should do things properly and, if we were going for a world record, everything needed to be above board. Ron Hendry made the point that if we went against the French instructions and then had a disaster, we might not have been covered by our insurance. It did still seem very unfair that we would have to row further than all the previous attempts.

I set about re-jigging the passage plan that, by this time, and with Geoff Cullington's able assistance, was growing into a very detailed document. Immediately we hit a snag. The original plan, without the extra three hours, worked neatly around the Thames and Seine tides. We could start the row at Westminster Bridge at slack water, just before the tide started to ebb and rush us down river to the estuary. The timing was such that we should then arrive at the mouth of the Seine just before the flood tide arrived to push us up the Seine.

The original plan also had a little leeway in it. We could have been up to two hours late arriving at the mouth of the Seine without losing the benefit of the flood tide to such an extent that we would not have been able to complete the 'daylight only' section.

Having to add three hours to the plan meant we would have to try to start before the tide ebbed in the Thames. This is difficult in many ways. Firstly, to start the row at Westminster Bridge the rowers had to get into the boat about a mile up river at the Westminster Boating base. They would have to row this first mile into the face of a still flooding tide and then a further two hours against this tide. This would sap their strength and lower their confidence. At sea, the rowers have no point of reference and cannot feel the effect of tide. In the river the tidal effect is painfully obvious.

We re-worked our computer model of the passage plan and I had another look at the hourly figures for the Amsterdam row. I noticed that there was a small discrepancy between the speeds recorded by my ship's log and those over the ground as calculated from hourly satellite-derived positions. This is actually quite normal, as the ship's log is mechanical and is manually calibrated. In very tidal waters such as the Channel Islands, it is difficult to achieve an accuracy of better than say a quarter or half a knot with this method. Anyway, the discrepancy on average was about 0.2 knot in our favour. Over the approximately 40 hours needed to get to Le Havre, it meant we might actually be a bit more than one hour better off than our original plan suggested.

On this basis, we set the new start time at two hours before high water at Westminster Bridge. Of course, all this relied on us being able to achieve the same or better average speed as previous rows and this would be very weather-dependent. To start talking about differences of 0.2 knot did seem a bit ridiculous, as no normal passage plan would attempt to work to such small tolerances. However, the Seine tidal window is so important that we had to get this right, and we had to know and appreciate the effect small differences in speed could have over the many hours of the row.

My new target for the row was now 84 hours. If we achieved this we would break the world record by 6.5 hours.

Budget

We had it in mind that we should try to raise more money than the Amsterdam row had and our early target was therefore to raise more than £20,000 for the MS Society. Our first shot at a project budget showed that the cost of mounting the row would be in the region of £25,000. In total, therefore, we would have to try and raise £45,000. This seemed like a huge mountain to climb, especially in comparison to the Amsterdam row, where costs were less than half that.

This time, we had a much larger team to support and organise over a greater period of time. Insurance, fuel and equipment costs would be much greater for this row. The huge target was daunting. Could we really contemplate raising so much money? It was David Read who gave us confidence and argued that really this was not impossible. Like most tasks, it becomes easier if broken into smaller pieces.

Fundraising, Marketing and PR

The committee developed a three-phase fundraising plan. Our first priority was to try to find a golden sponsor to hopefully underwrite the £25,000 costs of mounting the row. Without that sum we were dead in the water.

Our second phase was to try to gain corporate support from ideas such as sponsoring oars or from our 'Adopt a Rower' scheme.

Thirdly, we would appeal to the public of the Bailiwick of Guernsey and we decided to run a fundraising competition to help with this.

Having decided to develop a logo for the event, we solicited help from AWS Group, who had done so much for us for the last row. They very kindly agreed to take on all the merchandising and printing and design work for very little cost. They came up with a selection of logos and we put the various designs to the rowers to decide. Within a fortnight we had our logo and planned to use it on everything and it wasn't long before everyone in the island was familiar with the simple Eiffel Tower and Big Ben design.

A long list of local companies was drawn up and we set about approaching those where, in the first instance, we had some personal connection. A variety of approaches were tried, but we felt that an initial verbal contact was likely to be the most fruitful.

It actually took a few weeks before we made any progress. However, just prior to a meeting where I had been preparing to explain our lack of progress, I took a call from the MD of Premier Marinas, who came forward with a donation that set us on our way. The next few weeks saw a number of contributions coming forward.

All the committee members made contact with friends and acquaintances within businesses they knew in the island to try to find a 'golden sponsor'. Our idea here was to find one company to cover the £25,000 cost of actually doing the row. In exchange for that considerable sum, we hoped to be able to provide a huge amount of advertising via the island's media. It soon became clear, however, that we had chosen the wrong time of year to be asking for corporate money. Most of the companies we contacted wanted to help but had earmarked their charitable donations or sponsorship budgets months before.

Within our plan, we had recognised the need to get the media on our side as early as possible and we had decided that our PR efforts should proceed, with or without a main sponsor. A conversation I had with Rob Turville, a journalist at the Guernsey Press, threw another view into the ring, as he stated we were likely to get a much better reaction and far stronger media support if we were not trying to push a main sponsor's name all the time.

Other than working with PR agencies in our businesses, none of the committee members had direct experience of such work and we set about trying to find a local company who might help us. In addition, I made contact with a small firm based in London who I had used frequently in my past business. I knew Val and Jonica from Output Communicators could be relied on to help. They were most generous with their time and advice and immediately supplied an enormous list of media contacts in the U.K.

By coincidence, in early December I had a meeting at the Guernsey Yacht Club with Darren Duquemin from the advertising agency Wallace Barnaby to discuss a project I was working on for another charity and he kindly agreed to provide some free advice. It was a bit unprofessional of me, but I couldn't resist asking him to support the row project and even consider becoming our golden sponsor.

Darren graciously forgave my faux pas and said he would consider the matter and come back to me.

During this conversation Darren came up with an idea for the public launch of the London-to-Paris challenge. The Channel Islands' annual sporting awards are held alternately in Jersey and Guernsey. Darren reckoned that as this is one of the few events covered by live television in the islands and that it was guaranteed to be covered by all the media, we should try to make the announcement somehow at that event.

As Darren's agency was organising the event, he suggested he might be able to help. This was a scary prospect, as the awards were to be held at the end of January, just a few weeks away. We really wanted to have our sponsor in place by the time of the announcement.

A couple of days later Colin and I arranged to meet with Darren again, but this time we were to go to his offices. I hadn't worn a suit since I retired six years previously, but I thought I should in the circumstances. I arrived slightly early and in quite a bit of discomfort from, what were by now, rather snug fitting trousers. Colin screamed up on his bike wearing a tracksuit. 'Blimey mate – a suit,' Colin said. I was now a bit put out and feeling slightly foolish. 'Just because I am here begging doesn't mean I have to look like a tramp,' I said.

Darren couldn't persuade his board to become the project's main sponsor as, again, our timing was not right for them, but he confirmed he would speak to the sponsors of the sporting awards about announcing the row.

Just after Christmas Roger Martel was at the airport catching a flight to the UK and bumped into his friend Mike Ayre, MD at MeesPierson Reads. Roger mentioned the project and, while it clearly caught Mike's imagination, he warned from the start that his budget too was already allocated. Mike promised to consider Roger's request further and see if there was any way he could help.

About a week later Roger spoke to him again and Mike said that he might possibly be able to find half the amount we needed, but he would need to know more about the project to gain more support from within his organisation. This was an interesting dilemma for the organising committee because most of us wanted to grab the helping hand from MeesPierson Reads, but on the other hand, we still needed to find the other half of the money. If we persuaded Meespierson Reads to stump up half, would it jeopardise our chances of persuading other companies to come forward as a major sponsor? Also, what should we offer MeesPierson Reads in return for their sponsorship? Colin Fallaize had from the start been concerned that a golden sponsor might want too much from the project and that the golden sponsor's aims might clash with or suppress the main objectives of the row. Perhaps, then, a big sponsor who wasn't actually a golden sponsor might be better for the project. Could we possibly achieve that sort of balance?

Throughout January we kept plugging away at local businesses and maintained a dialogue with MeesPierson Reads. We had a number of near misses in finding our golden sponsor, but nothing solid materialised. All the while we were conscious that we ought to be progressing things, but also we didn't want to miss other opportunities.

The Plan

Meanwhile, we had been working on a number of other sponsorship deals for specific items such as the 3,500 gallons of diesel we would need for the guard boats. Total Oil had helped with past rowing events and we lost no time in knocking on their door this time.

General manager Tim Shepherd welcomed Roger Martel and me on our begging mission but was a bit taken aback by the size of our request. I must say even I had problems getting the words out. However, a shy, retiring wallflower Roger is not and, with no messing, he laid our cards on the table. We had another reason to see Tim: Total Oil was sponsoring the Channel Islands sports awards and we would need his help if we were to be allowed to make the announcement of the London-to-Paris challenge at the event.

A week or so passed and Tim got back to us to confirm that Total would supply all the fuel we needed. He also said he would arrange to help us with the announcement at the awards.

The day arrived and during the evening Colin was invited on to the stage to talk about the challenge. He was on good form and, according to many who attended, his contribution was one of the highlights of the evening.

I had prepared a press release and sent it out to all local media prior to the event, with an embargo until the morning after the awards. We had also arranged a press briefing, to be held at the yacht club. We waited anxiously for the media to arrive and then print journalists, radio presenters and TV reporters and cameramen streamed into the room.

The reaction to our announcement was fantastic and the entire front page of the local newspaper, the Guernsey Press, was devoted to the challenge. TV and radio coverage too, was impressive. The independent station, Channel TV, had interviewed a number of the rowers and the lads seemed to take to being on camera very easily.

The Plan

My favourite quote from the rowers came when Lloyd Le Page was asked how hard this was going to be. He answered: 'It is going to be very hard, tougher than anything we have attempted before, but it won't be as hard as living with MS.'

There was a burning need to try to get support from local ferry and airline companies. We would have to move a lot of people and equipment and we wanted to do this as cheaply as possible. I contacted Condor Ferries and was put in touch with Jane Livermore, who does their PR in Guernsey. I also contacted the Guernsey-based airline Aurigny, which immediately promised help where possible.

Jane is very proud and ferociously protective of the ferry company and I didn't perhaps get off on the right foot with her. I think she initially had the idea that we had approached Condor as a fall-back and that the airline was going to be our carrier of choice. In fact, we were hoping that Condor would help with moving people and equipment, but I explained that there could be a time advantage with using the airline, particularly for moving the people. The rowers actually chose to go on Condor because they could all travel together.

I bombarded Jane with booking plans, as we needed vehicles, trailers, boats, equipment and people moved at varying times to and from various places. Jane processed every request and, as some small return, the lads took part in a photo shoot rowing in Condor t-shirts. Jane also helped with the PR and freely gave me advice on local media releases.

We realised that specialist clothing for the rowers would be essential. Most of them had smart yellow breathable waterproof tops, courtesy of a previous challenge. These were good for wet and cold situations but would not be comfortable for the warm, dry conditions expected in the Seine. We needed to get hold of a number of specialist rowing shirts that would take moisture away from the body quickly. We found just the item we needed from a firm in Putney, but they would be very costly.

We pondered the cost and wrestled with the problem for a couple of weeks. Then, out of the blue, I took a call from Mark Shields at NRG International, saying that one of the community projects that they had sponsored for a number of years had fallen through. Mark said they had been following the rowers' progress and wondered if perhaps they could help us in any way. Suddenly, we had all the new clothing.

The urgency to find our main sponsor was now pressing. We had made the announcement of the event but still didn't actually have the funds to mount the row. We determined to progress things with MeesPierson Reads. It was clear that we had got Mike Ayre's attention, but we felt we needed to do more to convince him and others within the company that this was a project worth supporting and that the people involved in the project so far, were actually capable of putting the thing together. I also thought that MeesPierson Reads would need to be assured that they were not going to become involved in something that could become a PR disaster. In fact, Mike already knew Colin and a number of the other rowers, as he regularly used the Fitness Factory. He had also been aware of some of the past exploits undertaken on behalf of the MS Society.

It was agreed that the committee should make a presentation to MeesPierson Reads. In essence, we needed to put forward a sales pitch. Colin is never too comfortable with having to deliver a structured speech, preferring to speak from the heart. Other members of the team, me included, were rather happier to have planned what we were to say. This actually worked well, as Colin agreed to talk about the aims of the project and he spoke passionately about the plight of people in the island who have MS. By the time he had finished speaking, the team from MeesPierson Reads could not have failed to be convinced of the need for an MS nurse.

It was then left for us to explain how we intended to organise the row and to discuss how a main sponsor might benefit from association with the challenge. We also needed to convince our potential sponsors that we had the expertise and capability within the organising committee to actually mount the challenge. This last point was important to us. By that time, we felt strongly that our team should be responsible for all aspects of the organisation and that if a sponsor wanted to take over, or unduly influence the organisation, then there was a possibility that the aims of the project might change and become diluted or muddled.

By the time the meeting happened, the organising team had actually made an impressive start and the project plan had been fully developed and was on schedule. In planning our approach, we tried to imagine what our sponsor's major concerns might be and planned to highlight areas within our project plan designed to deal with these concerns.

It was obvious that PR and market awareness would be high on their list but we also felt they might be keen to know about our safety and contingency planning, as no sponsor wants to be involved with failure. We had to be honest about the dangers and difficulties of the event, but we hoped that, if our sponsor could be confident in our planning, then they too would find the associated risks to be acceptable. I felt that while we might very well fail to break the world record, it would not be a complete failure as long as everyone was safe.

The organising team went into this meeting expecting to have to work hard to convince MeesPierson Reads. We later learnt that they had already pretty well decided to come on board. For them, the meeting served to reinforce that decision and sort out the detail of their involvement.

We had been sent quite a long wish list and it was obvious that someone from our potential sponsor had been giving the project some thought. We felt comfortable with most of the wishes and had no problem agreeing to almost all of them. The one item that we were unhappy with was their request that we name the challenge 'The MeesPierson Reads London-to-Paris Row', or something similar.

By now, we were convinced that we would receive more support from the community and media if we did not feature our main sponsors name too prominently. Added to this, we felt that our potential sponsor might actually be getting too much for their money and that naming the project in this way might get in the way of our objectives. It turns out that this had been included more as a talking point than a demand and Mike and his team agreed with our thinking. The project remained the London-to-Paris MS Challenge.

Both sides left the meeting on a high. We knew that by adding this latest sponsorship to what we had raised elsewhere we would now have enough money to finance the row. The challenge was definitely going ahead and, from now on, every penny raised would go towards the MS nurse. We were on our way.

We decided to develop a system of strategically timed PR 'reminder' events. We looked through the project checklist and identified actions and events that might be of interest to the media. These included things like crew changeover practices in local waters and the story about the local prison being involved in the rowboat refurbishment. As each of these events came up, we sent out press releases and followed these up with calls to various journalists.

The Plan

Throughout the planning and preparation stages, a number of things happened that were newsworthy and we religiously publicised these to the media. The idea was for the project to be constantly in the public eye, with small news items being drip fed all the way along, punctuated with larger news items. The project was about raising money, but also awareness and we were confident that this strategy would achieve both. In the six months from start to finish the London-to-Paris row probably received more press attention in Guernsey than any charitable event had ever done.

Another part of our PR plan was to see if we could get a television company interested in following the project and to perhaps film the trip from the support boats. Warren Mauger from Channel Television had done just this on the Amsterdam row and we set about trying to persuade him to join us again.

Early on in our discussions Warren suggested doing a piece about living with MS for broadcast within the Channel Islands. Warren was keen to interview a number of people variously affected by the disease to stress the unpredictable nature of the problem, to explain why we needed an MS nurse and as a great way to introduce the idea of the row.

Warren interviewed three people on the Island, Danni Le Poidevin whose husband Steve had progressive MS, Nick Humphries whose life has been turned upside down by the disease and me. We all came out with pretty much the same messages and the short film made powerful viewing. Warren wanted to film me on my boat and arranged to get shots of me doing various nautical looking things and then he also wanted to carry out the interview on board. All went swimmingly for a while with shots of me looking over charts and fiddling with a compass and then we moved on to the interview. I have been interviewed a few times on camera before and am usually quite nervous; this time I was completely relaxed and very confident with the subject.

We were halfway through the interview when Warren asked: 'Why do we need an MS nurse on Guernsey?' I started my reply quite well, explaining that the disease usually appears in people's mid-30s, which meant that sufferers lived with it for a long time and that as the disease presented itself in so many different ways and in such a changeable manner, the care needed was very diverse.

I went on to say that our nurse would be there to co-ordinate the wide-ranging support needed. I started to explain also that the nurse would be there to provide help and support for the families of sufferers and, at this point my mind was flooded with memories of what Ros had gone through when she was told I had MS. I was completely overwhelmed with these thoughts and suddenly I was gulping for air and fighting back tears. This was so unlike me - I was sitting there sobbing uncontrollably and quite unable to speak. Warren graciously stopped the interview and promised not to use the footage of me blubbing.

A while later, Warren contacted me again to say that he was considering leaving Channel TV and setting up his own TV production company. He asked whether his first project could be to film the row. He then gave in his notice and set up Spike Productions with business partner and cameraman, Liam.

Warren and Liam filmed a number of practice sessions, interviewed various members of the team, and also filmed the organising committee during one of its many sessions. Three weeks before we were due to start the row, Spike Productions was asked to make a film about the work the Guernsey-based Mines Awareness Trust was doing in Kosovo. Warren and Liam reckoned they could pack all their gear, drive to Kosovo, get the footage they needed, avoid being blown up and get back to London in time to join the team for the start of the row. They made it pretty much by the skin of their teeth.

David Farrimond, bon viveur that he is, was convinced we should hold a fundraising dinner and thought that we might get support from a lot of the companies who had already helped in other ways. It was also a way of the team saying thank-you to our supporters. Being a retired caterer, I knew that planning and organising these events could be very taxing. I didn't want to pour cold water on the idea but must admit to keeping a low profile, rather than being much help with the event.

David and others worked like stink to sell the tables and arrange catering, lighting, entertainment and fundraising ideas for the night. The team decided to use the event to launch the third part of our fundraising master plan, which was the public competition. Somebody came up with the idea of using the 'Living with MS' feature filmed by Channel TV at the opening part of the evening.

I remember sitting watching this with David Farrimond and David Read a few days before the dinner was due to go off. It is quite a powerful and thought-provoking piece and as soon as it had finished I could see both Davids looking a bit uncomfortable. We had a long discussion about whether we should use it. Our main concern was that it might be a bit of a downer right at the beginning of the evening; on the other hand it was a great reminder of what the whole thing was about.

On balance, we thought we should go with it and screened the piece shortly after everyone had taken their seats. I had not sat down, choosing instead to stand at the back of the hall. I knew that if Ros could see me while the film was being shown, she was likely to be tearful.

When the piece ended there was absolute silence and I could see everyone looking sheepishly at everyone else, as if searching for other people's reactions before doing or saying anything. I decide to clap really loudly and for about three claps I was on my own, desperate for others to join in, then a thunderous applause started and continued for a long time. The gloom was lifted and the normal Channel Island cheer returned to the room.

The launch of the competition went well and the pledges of more money were very generous. Many companies who had adopted a rower also took a table and the adopted rowers each wore a polo shirt featuring the adopting company's logo together with our row logo.

The dinner was a good way to get the sponsoring companies and rowers together and I know that many of the companies started to develop a strong affinity for their adopted rower from that night.

By the day of the dinner we had already raised £55,000, which meant we had surpassed our original target and already had enough money to fund a nurse for a year. Colin and I had planned to speak after the dinner, a task neither of us relished. He spoke first and started with the line: 'Well, the good news is that we have now raised £30,000 for the MS Society and the really great news is that means we don't have to do the row.' Obviously this brought the house down, but, through the laughter, I am sure there were one or two people wondering if he really meant it. Then it was my turn to get up and do all the 'Thank-yous'. Normally I am pretty nervous, but it is amazing the difference it makes when you know your subject and, for once, I really enjoyed being up there in front of all those people.

The week of the dinner, Ros took a phone call from someone in the island whose telephone number is one digit different from ours. The chap calling said that a message had been left on his machine by mistake from someone pledging support for the row and he wanted to pass it on. Ros thanked him for taking the trouble and he said: 'No trouble, this is a subject close to our hearts. My son's girlfriend has MS and she is in a very bad way. We are all beside ourselves with worry. She is a lovely girl and my son loves her desperately, but we are so worried about the future. We are very supportive of the idea of the MS nurse and think this could help her parents who never get a break.' Ros spent another hour-and-a-half on the phone with this poor chap trying to be of some comfort and trying to help give some perspective at what was a very uncertain time.

Training

In addition to many hours of training on rowing machines, the rowers had a variety of other ways of getting ready for the challenge. While many enjoyed training together in the gym, some preferred to run the cliff paths or use rowing machines on their own.

However, fitness training was not the only form of training we had to be concerned about. I was very keen to communicate the information flowing from the group responsible for safety planning and to train all involved in the procedures that had been devised. We also needed to let everyone know about the logistics: to tell them, for instance, our plans for getting all the people, equipment and boats to London and then back from France and where everyone was to stay while in London and Paris. Even the simplest detail, such as exactly where the start was and where the finish was, had to be spelled out.

The number of people now directly involved in the project had grown to over 40 and we had to work out some way of conveying all this knowledge and to arrange some practice sessions. We decided to hold a health safety and information briefing at the yacht club and then to hold some safety training 'on water' where we would practise crew changeovers and other procedures such as 'man overboard'.

The Plan

The safety and information briefing was the first time the entire team had gathered and I remember being horribly nervous as we started the presentation. It didn't help that Dave Hadlington (Haddi), a member of Tristan's crew and a great mate of mine, giggled every time I looked at him and that the room was overly hot. I wasn't sure if he was giggling because he thought that I was talking rubbish, or if he just wanted to put me off. When I confronted him later he said he couldn't help laughing because apparently I had gone a funny red colour and looked ready to explode at any moment.

The meeting went off well, although the small team making the presentation had to go at quite a pace to cover everything in the time available. Perhaps as importantly as anything else, the whole team being together and discussing all the issues did, perhaps, highlight the sheer size of what we were undertaking. The meeting allowed the group to start to knit together as a cohesive team. A few rowers came up to me afterwards to say that they were very pleased to see the amount of work that had gone into safety planning, not so much because they were worried, but so that their wives, partners and family could be assured that every precaution was being taken.

The Sunday morning of the on-water practice dawned bright and still. I met some of Tristan's crew up at Beaucette Marina and, having got her ready for sea, we fired up the engines and made our way out of the Marina to head for St Peter Port. The sun was shining and the sea was incredibly calm. Although this made for lovely motor boating weather, I had hoped for some rather more challenging conditions in which to practice crew changeovers. Fifteen minutes later, we entered St Peter Port harbour and moored up alongside the massive granite structure of the old lifeboat slip. The rowers had all arrived and the film crew were there, interviewing various team members.

The Plan

When Colin made his team selection, he originally chose a crew of 16, plus he had also chosen a first reserve. 'The Swede' (Trevor Coulter) is actually Irish. However, when he first arrived on the Island, his accent was thought by one of his new work mates to be Scandinavian, and the name Swede has stuck with him ever since. The Swede was new to rowing, but was incredibly fit and had managed some amazing times on the rowing machine. His huge strength, gentle manner and determination endear him to everyone who meets him. He readily agreed to become first reserve and immediately slotted into the training programme. Almost as an aside Colin said while laughing: 'Only trouble is, the Swede isn't very good around water.'

'What do you mean?' I asked.

'Well, actually, he can't swim,' Colin said.

'Listen, Colin, I know we agreed that all things to do with the rowers were your responsibility, but this is a safety matter. Are you serious?' I asked.

Colin smiled one of his wry smiles.

'Relax, Rob... It's not a problem. In a few weeks, we'll have him swimming like a fish,' Colin replied.

Some weeks after Colin had made the decision about the Swede, he asked me if somehow we could fit him onto one of the support boats, even if he wasn't rowing. The big Irishman had put his heart and soul into the project and Colin couldn't bear the idea of him having nothing to show for his commitment. Even his swimming had improved no end. A couple of days after this conversation, Colin rang me to say that the decision had been taken out of our hands, as Mark Windsor had injured his knee badly while playing basketball; so badly that there was little likelihood that he would be able to row. The Swede would now take Mark's place.

As we tied Tristan up to the harbour wall, we could see the rowers gathering in several small groups around the model yacht pond. I could easily make out Mark, left leg bent and hobbling. We all felt terrible about his injury. Nobody had trained harder than he and, apart from his gammy leg, he was probably as fit as he had ever been.

I had got to know him on the last rowing challenge and we had got on well. Being a professional photographer, he was forever taking pictures of the rowers and we ended the Amsterdam row with a great photographic record. Mark has a quiet and focused approach to most things and he has a lovely sense of humour. But he wasn't laughing today. One of the first things Colin did in his briefing was to explain to the team that Mark would not be rowing. As he was talking, you could see Mark was trying to put a brave face on it, but we all knew how gutted he was. As usual with Colin, he found a brighter side and let the assembled group know that instead of rowing, Mark would now be joining us as official photographer. We had made our first substitution: it had to be our last, as we didn't have a second reserve.

It was time to stop the talking and get on the water for the practice exercises. By now, Roger with his boat Lecca Lecca, Buz and Access Challenger and the Rib drivers with the Boatworks+ Rib were all hovering in the harbour waiting for the rowers. We were all keen to try the changeovers with the Boatworks Rib, as some of the rowers were now wondering whether it was in fact too big for the task and that maybe it might be too high off the water.

We set of in convoy towards Havelet Bay where we would rendezvous with the rowing boat. As we reached Havelet it came screaming out of the bay heading south towards St Martin's point and the south coast of Guernsey. I looked around at the assembled fleet – it was really impressive. I felt that things were coming together.

A short while later I wasn't so sure. The lads had completed the first changeover and it had taken over two minutes. If we couldn't improve on that, it could mean spending two-and-a-half hours of the challenge just doing changeovers.

We spent the next two hours practising and although things became a bit tense with a lot of shouted commands and not a little swearing, slowly the times improved. By the end of the session, the rowers and boat crews had got it down to under a minute.

Not only was it the first time the rowers had transferred to and from the rowing boat and the big Rib, it was also a first for many of them to do the transfers from the Rib onto the larger support boats. Unlike the manoeuvre to and from the rowing boat, this one would always be carried out under way and, in the middle of the night with both boats pitching and rolling it called for steady nerves and skilful boat handling.

We rounded the afternoon off with man overboard practice. Adek had volunteered (half-jokingly) to jump into the water to make it more realistic, but I wouldn't let him, as the water temperature was only about 12 degrees. This was just as well, as our first attempt at picking up a fender and bucket was a complete farce. We discovered the Rib's radio was not working properly and the driver ended up trying to follow commands that came across like garbled Chinese whispers.

At the end of the session I was pleased with the overall result and even more convinced of the value of the practice. Apart from the radio, we were delighted with the Rib. The fears about its height and size had proved groundless and we were now convinced we could not have a better craft for the task.

The rowing boat and the Rib with film crew on board, during the first practice session.

Some of the Row team: from left to right, John Lewis, Robbie Beck, Mark Windsor, Mark Shepherd, Sam de Kookier, Colin Fallaize, Steve Pipe ("Pipey"), Geoff Van Katwyk (Rib driver),

From left to right, Karl Pederson, Sam de Kooker, Colin Fallaize, Trevor Coulter ("The Swede") Adrian de Kooker

Guard boat "Tristan"

Guard boat "Access Challenger"

Guard boat "Lecca Lecca"

The Boatworks Rib

Final checks

Some items on our checklist, like sorting out details of
the finish, could only be achieved by travelling to France
and by carrying out physical checks.

David Farrimond and I were keen to get to Paris to sort
out a number of issues and my good friend Mark Dravers
offered to fly us there in his four seater plane. We had
planned an early start, as we had a lot accomplish that
day. We wanted to meet up with the Paris branch of the
MS Society. We also needed to arrange a reception in
Paris and accommodation for the rowers. In addition, I
wanted to check out the finish and make sure we had a
plan for getting the rowboat out of the water and then to
get all the support vessels berthed nearby. We also had to
arrange a fuel supply, which is notoriously difficult on the
Seine.

My alarm went off at 5.00am. I looked outside and it
was dark, grey and damp. I called Mark at home. He
wasn't hopeful of being able to take off because of fog and
low cloud. We waited until seven, but in the end, had to
postpone the trip.

A week later, with much clearer weather, we were off.
We met all the objectives for the trip, but there was one
major problem. When we arrived at the Seine I could not
believe the speed of the current. The previous week's rain
had swollen the river and we reckoned the current was
perhaps four or five knots. At this height, it would be
completely un-rowable.

On top of this roaring current, the river traffic was truly
frightening and my apprehension grew when I saw the
enormous push barges and 'bateau mouches' charging
downstream at over 10 knots. This vision was to come
back and haunt me later.

The river was so swollen that the pilothouses of the
push barges were too high to get under the bridges.

Amazingly, these are designed to raise or lower hydraulically so that bridges can be navigated. These monsters would tear downstream towards our finishing bridge and, at the very last moment, lower the pilothouse to get under. Of course, while the pilothouse is in its lower position the barge's skipper cannot actually see ahead as his vision is completely obscured by the barge and its cargo. I kept imagining what would happen if the hydraulics failed.

The river level was a big worry. Our first possible go date – the date on which the attempt was to start from Westminster Bridge – was only two weeks away. We spoke to the department who monitor the levels and flows on the Seine to see what their view was. Their advice was that the level could drop almost as quickly as it could rise and that as this latest rise was due to short, sharp rains, they didn't expect the levels to remain high for long. This obviously relied on there being no further rain in the vast catchment area of the Seine and its tributaries.

Roger Martell and David Read, in particular, were very anxious about this development and they seemed to gain little comfort from the projections of the river authorities. I did what I could to placate them and gave daily information on river levels. There seemed little point in adding to the tension with my own worries about general weather conditions, which I felt, statistically, were far more likely to be our undoing.

The skippers of each boat were tasked with counter-checking and signing off the equipment list of each other's boats. We went through everything. We checked we had spare bulbs, filters, nuts, bolts, belts and screws. We checked that every extinguisher was in date, that all lifejackets and life rafts had been serviced, and that the correct flares were on board and were in service date. The checklist was endless, but worth doing, as one or two discrepancies were picked up and sorted out.

The plan

I went to check Buz's boat, which took ages. It took a long time, not because there was anything wrong, but because it is a fascinating boat and Buz has a story to tell about every piece of her. This isn't surprising, really, as Buz built her himself, from a burnt-out hulk. Long after the challenge was over, Warren wrote a piece in the local paper about his time on the challenge and he described the discomfort of sleeping in Buz's oily engine room. This was a bit of poetic licence, really, to liven up the tale, but I think you probably couldn't find a bigger insult for Buz! He was furious and protested loudly that his engine room was the cleanest in the Channel Islands.

Chapter seven - Decisions, decisions

A weak man has doubts before a decision; a strong man has them afterwards

Karl Kraus

Geoff Cullington was busy working on the navigation and we spent a number of weeks bouncing ideas and plans forwards and backwards by email. Geoff had identified the critical points of the voyage and the most significant of these was the need to navigate the lower section of the Seine during daylight hours. This is a legal requirement and it was this single factor that dictated the rest of the passage plan. The strong ebb and flow of the Seine is notorious and it was obvious to us that we needed to be at the mouth of the river at the beginning of a flood tide. Actually, I don't think that those who had previously made attempts at the record really understood this, the most critical requirement of the passage plan. The time of high water gets later the further up the river you go, and high water in Rouen is actually four hours later than at Le Havre. In theory, if the rowers could row fast enough, we could have as many as ten hours of flood tide to push us towards the first lock. I say *if* the rowers can row fast enough, because the tide is like an escalator that you fall off unless you are going fast enough. Worryingly, morning flood tides occur only during spring tides[7] and this would increase the tidal flow in the channel and the possibility of larger waves. I calculated we had a window of about four days after the start of each spring tide cycle which would give us sufficient daylight in which to complete the

---

[7] Spring tides occur when the moon, earth and sun are in alignment (twice a month). The increased gravitational pull on the sea produces larger tides. The smaller tides which result from the moon, earth and sun not being aligned are called neap tides.

'daylight only' section of the Seine. The first available spring tide on 31st May would also offer us the advantage of a full moon.

Within the committee there had been much discussion about when we should attempt the row. Some felt that a September go date would give us a much better chance of being organised on time and of raising the required cash. There was also concern that melt water from the Alps might affect the level of the Seine in May and could make the row impossible.

In past events, it was always sea conditions and waves that had hampered or stopped the row.

We asked Jersey Met for advice and they trawled through 10 years of records of significant wave heights in the channel and came up with statistics that made the decision for us. With the months of July and August discounted because of holiday and other commitments, May and June were clear winners. In June, wave heights are less than 1m for 60% of the time. In September this figure drops to 40%.

We discovered a website that gave daily statistics on the level of the Seine. We now felt we now had enough sources of information from which to make a decision on when to go. Logistically, though, this decision was to be a nightmare.

Our first possible go date had been set as the Bank Holiday Monday 31st May. The French authorities actually wanted us to plan to arrive in the river on this day as they preferred to have us going up the Seine on a day when there would be little commercial traffic. To start on 31st, the support boats would need to leave Guernsey on the Friday.

We planned to make the first decision as to whether or not the support boats would go as planned on the Wednesday morning. By this time, the media in Guernsey had really got hold of the story and my phone was near melting point. Everyone wanted to know if the start was going ahead as planned.

By Monday 24th the weather forecasts were looking decidedly dodgy. Nothing much changed by the decision-making day of Wednesday. The forecast for our start date was for a south-westerly force 5, possibly 6, but confidence in the forecast was pretty low.

A start on Bank Holiday Monday looked very unlikely. The rowing boat was booked on the ferry to England on that day and we decided to let it go, just in case the weather improved.

Tony Cullington was to tow the boat initially to a relative's house in Hertfordshire, where it would sit safely in a meadow before being taken to London, 24 hours before the start. All through our planning we had been concerned that if something happened to the rowing boat on its way to England, we had to allow time either to repair it, or to get a replacement vessel over from Guernsey. With this in mind, Tony set off, safely delivering the boat to the meadow and then returned to Guernsey.

On Wednesday we released a statement to the press, explaining that the row was to be delayed. By now, my phone had taken on a life of its own, and I sat at my computer at home taking calls on two land lines and my mobile and trying to deal with email number 963. We had agreed a system to spread news to rowers and support staff, but most of the 50 people involved had questions that weren't answered by it, or had yet another suggestion for a useful weather website.

There was a glimmer of hope that the weather for the next week might allow us a start by the Thursday. It was a long shot. Two of the three weather computer models I was using agreed that a high could come in by the Thursday, but all three stated that confidence in these forecasts were low. I felt this was not enough to commit the team to going to London and was worried that if we didn't take this opportunity, there was no guarantee that the weather for the next set of go dates would be any better.

Roger Martell and David Read were still concerned about the level of the Seine. While it had dropped considerably, they were worried that the next expected rains over the weekend could make it flood again. Also, while there could be more settled weather at the end of the week, the support boats would probably have a very unpleasant trip over on the days prior to the better conditions arriving.

Somewhere along the way, the idea developed that maybe, just maybe, we could have two bites at the cherry. Would it be possible to take all the boats, rowers and support crews over to London for a possible start on the Thursday, only to find we had to postpone it at the 11th hour? Could we actually then arrange to bring them all back two weeks later? Could everyone negotiate time off work? Would all the boats be available and would Condor Ferries help us? Did we all actually have the stomach for it?

Geoff Cullington was in Scotland halfway through a round-Britain cruise that he had already very generously agreed to abandon as soon as the go was announced – could I really ask him to contemplate doing that twice?

I cannot imagine entertaining this sort of plan anywhere else but Guernsey. I just had a feeling that the islanders might at least hear the plan out. Within 24 hours all those involved with the project had been asked about the idea and, amazingly, every single person had pledged his or her support to the two-bite strategy.

Chapter seven: *Ros' story*

You don't expect this kind of thing is ever going to happen to you – Rob getting MS, that is. And I'm from a family where nobody is ever ill.

When Rob started experiencing the numbness that was his first symptom, I was worried, but I didn't think it was MS. I was thinking of a stroke or maybe a tumour.

When he got the diagnosis, he didn't give me a 'sit down, I've got something to tell you' sort of thing – there was no drama – but I was very shocked and scared. Immediately an image of a wheelchair came into my mind. Then, even though the girls were very young at the time, for some reason I had the thought that if they got married, Rob wouldn't be able to walk them down the aisle.

When the terrible headaches started, I was confused – I wasn't sure if it was MS or the effects of the lumbar puncture.

Since then I've been learning to live with the unknown, seeing him suddenly vulnerable and knowing that this is what we would have to deal with for the rest of our lives.

Early on, Rob went to a medical library to look it up and I said: 'What did you want to do that for?'

'To find out the whole scenario,' he said. He wanted to know exactly how bad it might be and what it might involve.

I didn't. I thought there was no point. I also felt helpless, because I couldn't do anything.

I would have given anything for him not to have it: I'd have gone and lived in a box if he just didn't have it.

But Rob has never shown any sign of feeling sorry for himself and I really admire him for that.

We decided not to try to explain the full seriousness of Rob's condition to the girls immediately. Neither of us wanted to frighten or worry them and, anyway, at that stage we didn't really know too much ourselves. They were so young that it was possible to pass symptoms off as something else, and Rob worked such long hours that often he was up and out before they woke up and didn't get home again until they were asleep, so even when he was in hospital, we could make light of it.

As time progressed, though, Rob was determined not to hide things from them.

He wanted to slowly and matter-of-factly introduce the reality of MS. I was not completely comfortable with this, but perhaps that was just me being very protective. I'm still not sure what the best approach is and think that, to an extent, it may vary according to the girls' differing personalities. The MS Society now produces much better literature designed to explain these things to children.

If you can be said to be blessed, when something like this happens, the blessing has been having Rob at home more than he would have been if he'd carried on working.

We're fortunate that so far the disease hasn't been as debilitating for him as it could have been – although I'm very aware that that could change at any time.

Fortunately too, he could afford to stop working. He sold the business and, though we are not fabulously wealthy, we're okay financially.

With Rob having retired, we started to think about where we were living. The sea is so important to both of us – this book tells you all you need to know about Rob's passion for boats and I'd grown up on the coast at Mumbles in Swansea Bay. Our landlocked Buckinghamshire village, as beautiful as it is, wasn't going to be right for us in retirement. Our lawyer gave us a long list of places that would make economic sense and we picked Guernsey. It's not too far away and Rob had been before and loved it. I quickly came to see it as a lovely place for the girls to grow up. We needed to make a fresh start and go forward together, yet we were giving up our support network in the UK.

Fortunately, within a year of arriving in Guernsey we had made some great friends and found a house to make our home – an old farmhouse in the centre of the island, which needed a bit of work, but once we had done that it was perfect for us.

Chapter eight - Next stop: Brighton

On Friday 29th May, we confirmed that the guard boats would leave the island on the Monday. This left us a couple of days to make sure all the equipment was loaded and the safety checklist had been completed.

The Co-Op in Guernsey had supplied the rowers' food and we made arrangements for theirs and that of the crews, together with all the rowers' gear, to be brought on board the guard boats. In total, we would be carrying enough for 700 meals. A steady stream of rowers and their families turned up with food, equipment, clothing and bedding. While this was happening to Tristan in Beaucette Marina in the north of the island, similar scenes were unfolding on board guard boats Lecca Lecca and Access Challenger in the marina in St. Peter Port. Girlfriends and wives of the rowers congregated on Tristan's flybridge, while we tried to stow everything.

I had learnt from the last row that we needed to be much more organised in our stowing and I had managed to find three tiers of plastic stacking drawers for the food. These were lined up in the galley along the main companionway and were fastened to the bulkhead by bungee cord attached to giant suction cups normally used to hold fishing rods on the roof of a car. A chain was formed to pass the food below and it seemed to be never-ending. I think every baked bean and tin of stewed steak, can of 'Big Breakfast' and packet of dried potato and pot noodle in Guernsey was now on board Tristan. Even the 12 huge drawers and Tristan's normal galley storage were not enough, and more space had to be found in the forward accommodation. Years later I was still coming across the odd tin of 'Big Meal' soup and packet of Jaffa Cakes in the most unlikely places.

In addition, homes had to be found for box after box of bottled water and high energy drinks. People kept turning up, but nobody seemed to leave. Eventually we had about 20 people on board. With 500 gallons of diesel, 150 gallons of water and heaven knows what weight in high-carb food and drink, Tristan was sitting very low in the water. I was getting bit concerned about the boat's stability and finally had to stop anyone else coming on board.

We eventually had everything squared away and well secured and, as evening arrived, Tristan's crew went over everything one last time. Among the final pieces of kit to be brought on board were all the oars and Dave Hadlington's diving gear and tanks. Two of the guard boats were equipped with diving gear and there were any number of qualified divers among the crew. It is depressingly common to come across discarded fishing net in channel waters. We were determined that if our propellers were to become fouled, we should at least have a fighting chance of clearing them.

The support boats' journey to London was to take two days. Premier Marinas had arranged free berthing for the boats at Brighton. It was our intention to arrive in London at least 24 hours before the rowers, to allow time to fix any mechanical problems. Also, the final decision to get the rowers over to England was to be made from London only when we knew we had a clear weather window. We also had to be sure that the flow of the Seine was acceptable and that all boats and equipment were working correctly.

This 24-hour gap was indeed useful, as we discovered Access Challenger needed a software upgrade to her navigation system in order to use the latest charts, and Roger needed a new part for his radio. By amazing coincidence, Robin Ayre of Radio Electronics, Guernsey, who had provided electronic charts free of charge for the event, happened to be in London and, at a moment's notice, dashed over to fit the parts and upgrades.

Next stop Brighton

To get the most of the north-going tide, Tristan, the Boatworks Rib and Access Challenger met off Beaucette Marina at the north end of the Little Russell channel in between the Islands of Guernsey and Herm at 5am on Monday 31st May. It was a cool morning and the weak grey light added to the chill. It was an odd feeling as the boats met up in this monochrome seascape. It felt a bit like we were in some black and white film; we could have been commandos going on a dawn raid.

Lecca Lecca, being much faster than the other boats, was to set off later and rendezvous in Brighton. The forecast was not great, but at least the projected force 5 winds would be behind us. The actual conditions were rather different to forecast and this became a mark of the entire trip. In the end, the winds on the way to Brighton were much lighter and we had an enjoyable 'boysey' trip. Lecca Lecca caught up and passed us with about 20 miles to go. We arrived about 10 minutes later than Lecca Lecca and were instructed to berth all the boats alongside. We called for someone on board Lecca Lecca to take a line, but she was already deserted. Her crew was sinking a pint in the nearest pub – this, too, was to become a normal occurrence during the trip.

Apart from the early morning and the times when we were out of range of telephone masts, my phone was ringing constantly. So many people were now involved in some way with the challenge and everybody seemed to want information. I was really pleased to be getting loads of calls from the media as this meant our PR was working well. From that day on, it seemed that either Colin or I, and sometimes both of us together, were being interviewed for the newspapers, radio or TV. The wonders of modern technology would allow our many followers and supporters in Guernsey to follow our every move, and to share our highs and lows.

Next stop Brighton

The trip from Brighton to London was fairly uneventful and we used the journey up the Thames to check our proposed navigation out of the estuary. It can be exited via any one of five, finger-like, channels. The southernmost of these, the Four Fathoms channel, is, as the name suggests, shallow and usually used only by small fishing vessels and leisure boats. We had intended to use it, as it would provide the shortest route and take us away from commercial shipping. We would be navigating it at low water and, when we checked the available depths, we found we had less water than the charts suggested. To add to the difficulty, navigation of this channel required adherence to a very narrow course. Buz, skipper of Access Challenger, and Big Stuey, first mate, were concerned that negotiating this channel at night could be too risky and was an unnecessary risk. I agreed that we should consider our alternatives and Stuey set about shaping a new course.

We had arranged to berth in London at Limehouse Marina, which, at the time of booking, was run by the Cruising Association. The association had been very accommodating and had agreed a peppercorn berthing charge for the four support vessels. A couple of weeks earlier, I had called the marina to see if we could launch the rowing boat at Limehouse and found that Thames Water had taken over the marina. The new staff knew nothing about us.

Having checked their records, they agreed to honour the berthing agreement, but arrangements for the rowboat had to be made elsewhere. Then, two days before we were due to leave Guernsey, we received a call to say that their swing bridge was stuck in the closed position and that it would not be fixed for two weeks. Although that was bad news for us, it was even worse for the sailing rally that was now stuck in the marina. Roger Martel offered to look at the problem.

Next stop Brighton

I had considered St Katherine's Marina and had discounted it because the tidal window to get in and out each day was a bit short. A member of staff at St Katherine's offered Roger a special lock opening for the start day which would ensure we could get all vessels in position below Westminster Bridge. This was excellent news, as St Katherine's is nearer the start and was an easier location in which to rendezvous with the rowers and other support team members.

St Katherine's even offered to match the deal that Limehouse had offered, so this move would not dent our budget. St Katherine's was also convenient, as the fuel barge *Burgan* with whom we had negotiated a good deal for 800 gallons of diesel, was berthed just downstream of the marina.

As we entered the estuary on our way up to St Katherine's, we realised that if we got a move on, we could get fuelled up before we locked into the marina. That would save us having to exit and re-enter it the next day. We had been told that there was no speed limit in the lower section of the Thames but decided to radio the Port of London Authority to check. They confirmed that there was no limit, but asked us to keep our wash down when passing moored craft. Minutes later Lecca Lecca was flying up the ever-narrowing Thames at 35 knots. We all managed to get 'fewled arp' by our new Cockney mates on the fuel barge *Burgan*. We were then entertained with some exciting boat-handling opportunities provided by the current screaming past the entrance to St Katherine's dock. While not particularly used to rivers, the skippers of the support boats were all very accustomed to stemming the very strong currents around the Channel Islands and, for them, this entrance was not a problem.

A number of others were not so fortunate as to possess this experience and we watched with a mixture of smugness and concern as a number of craft aimed for the lock entrance only to find themselves disappearing downstream and on a course to collide with our boats which were moored to the waiting buoys below the entrance.

Everyone managed to enter the lock without damage, other than bruised egos, and soon we were secure inside the wonderfully exciting and picturesque marina. Lecca Lecca was, again, in first, and by the time I was shutting down Tristan's engines Lecca Lecca was already looking like the Mary Celeste. Lecca Lecca's crew was carrying out a provisioning recce in the Dickens Inn.

The rowers were all set to get on the ferry the next morning and the time was upon us to make the final decision as to whether or not to proceed. I consulted the computer for the latest weather forecasts and double checked things with the Jersey and UK Met Offices by phone. Jersey Met had given me a link to five computer models and, these, too, were studied. There were differences in all the forecasts, but all but one of the computer models showed that there should be an opportunity for a start on Thursday. Unfortunately, the one thing all the forecasts still agreed on was that the confidence level of their predictions was low.

I was acutely aware that if we did not take this opportunity, then there was no guarantee that there would be good enough weather during our next set of possible go dates in two weeks' time. I got on the phone to Colin, and with butterflies in my stomach, confirmed that the rowers should indeed board the ferry to Weymouth in the morning.

The next morning the first thing we did was to check the forecasts. While we were studying the computer screen there was a knock on the hull. The harbourmaster of St Katherine's dock had come to introduce himself.

'I just wanted to say that I have instructed the staff to help you guys in any way they can and that you are not to be charged a penny for your stay here. What you are doing is fantastic,' he said.

I thanked him for his tremendous welcome and we talked about the amazing reaction we had received wherever we went.

'It is not surprising,' he said. 'MS is a disease that touches so many people.'

At that point his voice broke and his eyes welled up. He struggled to get his next sentence out. 'My wife has progressive MS.'

He went on to explain how the disease had developed into the progressive type fairly recently and how this had been a devastating blow to them both. He was now at a point where he was contemplating retirement so that he could spend more time with his wife.

The rest of the day was spent getting fresh provisions on board the guard boats and making final checks of our engines and equipment. The Rib crew rigged up the big piece of carpet which was to be draped over the port sponson to stop the gates on the rowboat from damaging or even piercing it. The Jersey team had suffered precisely that problem mid-channel and lost the use of one of their Ribs. Now that we had decided not to use the four fathoms channel, I had to make appropriate alterations to the passage plan. With big Stuey's help, we shaped a course that would take us just on the outside of the southern edge of the Queen's Channel, which is one of the routes used by the large ships. While this added about one-and-a-half miles to the journey, we could at least be confident that we would have sufficient depth under our keels. I had to print out copies of the new passage plan, which, by now ran to about five pages, and that job alone took two hours as I wrestled to connect to a printer that the hotel next to the marina had let us use.

In among all these happenings, my phone was still ringing constantly with a continual stream of journalists,

TV people, rowers and helpers calling for information or checking details. One of these calls was from a journalist from one of the national newspapers. This lady, with a cut-glass accent, called to say she was on London Bridge and couldn't see anything. Should she be on a pontoon and had she missed the start? We had sent out very precise and detailed information to the press. I couldn't help giggling as I told her that the good news was she hadn't missed the start, but the bad news was that she was on the wrong bridge on the wrong day.

Late in the afternoon, we heard that the rowers had arrived safely in the accommodation provided by the London Goodenough Trust in Mecklenburgh Square and that they were all about to go out for 'a last supper'. The boat crews, too, took the opportunity to grab a good meal before getting a reasonably early night.

Just before going to sleep I went over the project checklist, the safety plan and the equipment lists one last time. I knew if I didn't do that, I would not sleep. The only thing we had to do in the morning was a last water top-up and check that the various parties of rowers and boat crews were in the right place at the right time.

Chapter nine - Good to go

Thursday morning came and the first thing we did was check the forecasts. There were no real changes from the day before and the predictions at that point were for NE force four dropping to almost nothing, with the chance of light westerly or south-westerly winds developing on Friday. The NE wind for our journey back down the estuary was not ideal, but the rowers would be fresh, and were confident they could handle it. I radioed the Port of London Authority to advise them that conditions looked good for a one o'clock start and to check for any unusual river movements or hazards that we should be aware of.

The morning's plan quickly unfolded into reality. Two of the Rib crew went by taxi to the Westminster boating base where they were met by staff from the base and taken by boat up to Putney to collect the rowing boat. From there they were to tow it downstream to Westminster. A party of rowers had gone to Putney to fix in the seats, radar reflector and other equipment that had been removed for transportation and then they helped launch the boat. Meanwhile, the first rowing crew went to the Westminster boating base to await the arrival of the rowing boat.

The time came for all four support boats to enter the lock for the special opening that had been arranged for us. At a little after 11 am, all the boats were making their way up to Westminster Bridge. The Rib was the only vessel to go further than that, as it was to meet up with the rowing boat, deliver the oars that had been transported on Tristan and escort the rowers to the start. The other three support boats crossed over to the right bank, downstream of the bridge, and hovered right by the London Eye, trying to keep out of the way of the river traffic. We were in radio contact with the shore team, who by now had gathered on the bridge. The team on the bridge were in constant contact with Doctor Gee, the official timekeeper, and it was their job to let him know the precise moment the bow of the rowing boat emerged from under the bridge. The doctor was then to start his stopwatch and record the start time.

We had about half an hour to wait before the rowing boat was due to reach the bridge and on board Tristan there was a peculiar atmosphere. I suppose it was nervous tension; the minutes went by slowly, with the odd joke interspersed with long periods of silence. The boats constantly manoeuvred to stem the tide. I looked at the heavy flow of water still rushing upstream, constantly piling up and falling sideways from the piers of the bridge. Had we got this wrong? Could the lads actually row against this?

At about twenty to one Tony Cullington radioed from the bridge that the rowing boat and the Rib were in sight. They seemed to be making very slow progress and I really wondered if they would get to the start at all. We snatched occasional glimpses of the rowers in the distance and, little by little, they came closer and closer. We had received instructions that the rowers had to use the middle span of the bridge, but of course that was where the maximum flow was.

At four minutes past one, they emerged from under the bridge and the sound of cheering from the supporters on the bridge reached us, and all the boat crews joined in.

Four minutes late in starting, the rowers were really working hard. Their speed through the water must have been nearly seven knots, but over the ground they were barely making 3 knots. As soon as they could, the rowers made their way as far over towards the right bank as possible, to get out of the current. Then, in what seemed to be only minutes, they had to come out into the middle again in order to get around HMS Belfast, which is moored just upriver of the Tower of London.

Good to go

Mark Windsor snapped a brilliant shot of the rowing boat, the Belfast and Tower Bridge and sent it over the Internet to the Guernsey Press. The picture took up the whole of the next day's front page. From then on, Mark spent the entire trip either taking photos or sitting at the computer on board Tristan, sorting and sending a huge number of them. His dedication was certainly worth it, as his book later to be published in Guernsey proved.

The computer station was popular with Warren, too, as he had arranged to keep a weblog on the challenge site that he updated throughout the row. During the row, islanders were urged to send messages of support by text that would also be shown on the web. As well as boosting the morale of the rowers, it brought a few welcome pounds to the kitty.

The river was rushing past the Belfast and the flow of water past her huge mooring buoys was worrying. The rowers were just lining up to past the ship when they were hit by the wake from a ferry. They missed a stroke and the boat was forced up onto one side, but in a moment, the boys settled it and Lloyd, who was in stroke, urged them back into rhythm. I took comfort from the way they completed the movement with such ease and calm; it was a small demonstration of just how accomplished they were as rowers.

The first hour had nearly passed and the time had come to do the first changeover. We were coming up to Convoy's Jetty, precisely where the passage plan suggested we should have been. The Rib dropped back from its position just aft of the rowing boat, and slipped alongside Lecca Lecca, to pick up the next five rowers. A crew from Tristan had started the challenge and now it was the turn of the Lecca Lecca men to take over.

We had perfected the changeover manoeuvre during practice and now carried it out under way, with just a line from the bow of the Rib going to a forward cleat on the guard boat. With the new team on board the Rib, they made their way back to the rowing boat and signalled the rowers to stop. As it slowed, it was hit by a large wake and rocked violently from side to side. Lloyd shouted: 'Ah hell, the bloody rudder has jumped off,' and sure enough it was floating behind the boat, dangling from its control cable. John Lewis, the incoming stroke, stretched over the stern of the rowing boat and quickly replaced the rudder in its pintles. We were left wondering how long it would stay there. We realised there should have been a locking mechanism, but it was too late to manufacture one now. Having completed the crew change, the boys from Lecca Lecca powered up and, with the last of the flood tide weakening, started to pick up speed.

***

The rowers being interviewed by Sky TV before the start.
From left to right: Adek de Kooker, Trevor Coulter, Sam de Kooker, Karl Pederson

Seconds after the start at Westminster Bridge

Hit by a large wake, the rudder comes off

The Rib, now with the Tristan rowing crew on board, turned around, passing Lecca Lecca, on their way back to Tristan. The lads leapt aboard Tristan, dripping sweat, and gathered on the aft deck.

'I thought we were never going to get to the start,' said Sam.

'Yeah, the RIB could've towed us to the start – that would have saved us rowing a mile against that tide,' said Lloyd. 'Did you see how much tide there was?' How are we doing, Rob?'

Lloyd Le Page is a stalwart of the rowing club and, while he is one of the smallest and lightest members of the team, his technical skill and fitness make up for his size. Lloyd is also a calming influence. His work leading a team of electrical engineers needs a cool head, a clear thinker and good communicator. Answering Lloyd, I just said: 'We are doing fine, bang on where we should be.'

Karl Pedersen, constantly smiling, and one of life's 'glass is half full' types, just said with a laugh: 'I'd never seen the London Eye before. Now I've seen that, the Houses of Parliament, Tower Bridge and the Tower of London - and all from our own boat. What a change to be rowing on a river. These river rowers don't know what real rowing is.'

Dave Hadlington's head popped through the saloon door, 'Kettle's on: who's for tea?'

A little further along the river we passed the Royal Naval College at Greenwich. This place bought back masses of memories for me. During my time with Sutcliffe Catering, the Naval College had been amongst the portfolio of London clubs for which I had overall responsibility. I didn't have time to linger over these memories, though, as the boys soon powered past its vast grand frontage and on, past Hookness Point and Bow Creek entrance, towards the huge structure of the Thames barrier.

We had to slow slightly as a passenger liner made its way through the barrier, its massive slab sides towering over the ridiculously tiny rowing boat. It was now time for the second crew changeover and we decided not to carry it out until after we had cleared the barrier. I had called Woolwich radio, who control all river traffic through the barrier, and, with their permission, passed safely between two of the enormous piers. We tucked over to the side of the river again and prepared ourselves for the next changeover.

Colin winked at me and gave me one of his big grins as he and the other four rowers readied themselves to board the Rib. I knew he was relishing this moment. It would be his first hour-long session of what could be as many as 40 such stints over the next few days. He and the other rowers had been desperate for this day to arrive. They had become bored with practice, but the thought of this moment had kept them all at the training grindstone. Colin just wanted to get into that boat with his team and make it fly. Even at this point of excitement, though, his focus was still on the team. He ushered them along, checking small details and cracking jokes.

'Come on lads!' he said, 'Get a move on. The Lecca Lecca boys have really had to work hard and remember: they've been rowing well over their hour now. We can't let them down by being late for the changeover.'

Good team captain that he was, having checked that the rest of the session's team were safely aboard the Rib, he was the last to leave Tristan.

The crew changeover was completed quickly and without fuss and, moments later, the Rib cruised past us on its way back to Lecca Lecca to deposit the outgoing crew for a well-earned break. As they went past, Andy Chapple shouted out: 'How did we do there?' Andy was one of our most experienced rowers, one of three in the team who had rowed across the Atlantic.

'We're doing fine,' I replied. 'Right on schedule.'

I was glued to my copy of the passage plan, which showed a predicted time of arrival at dozens of points along the river. However, I was careful not to give out too much information about our progress and would simply say that we were 'on schedule' or 'doing fine'. There were many reasons for this and early into the planning I had decided that while general words of encouragement would be useful, too much worrying about, or indeed contentment with any position within the first two days of the row would be foolish. If I gave out hourly positions then it might develop into a race between crews and the rowers could lose sight of the overall objective.

Pete Goss tells a lovely story illustrating this point. On one Atlantic crossing, where food is always important, Pete offered the incentive of a Mars bar to the fastest watch in a day. The two watches carefully scrutinised and recorded the distance sailed during each shift. Some while later, Pete realised he had made a mistake when he discovered the watches were actually de-tuning the boat just before handing over to the next watch!

***

Adek de Kooker front of picture, Colin Fallaize in the blue headband - pulling hard.

The sea piles up on the second day.
From left to right: Andy Chapple. Colin Robert. Mark Shepherd. Robbie Beck. Joe Paul

Our plan was based on estimated positions, which would be affected by so many variables. The most important checkpoint was the mouth of the Seine and if we reached it within an hour or two of the plan then I would know that there was a real chance of breaking the record. I started to gain a little more confidence as we reached each point on the river within minutes of the planned times.

I had visualised each section of the passage so many times that it was strange now to be replacing my made-up images of places with the real thing. Convoy Jetty, West India Pier, and Hookness Point all took on real form as we approached. Two hours into the row, we had changed crews twice. It was at this point that the tide started to change and the scenery was now going past more rapidly.

The lower Thames is not pretty. Its waters are full of debris and litter and its banks are lined with the decaying legacy of numerous unused wharfs and jetties. The dilapidated piles were like rotting teeth in the filthy mouth of this river. I wondered if the lower reaches of the Seine would be similar.

By five pm we had reached Gravesend and completed four crew changes. With nearly three knots of current we were achieving 8 or 9 knots over the ground. Very quickly the riverbanks seemed to be further away. We were eating up the miles and rapidly approaching the estuary. Sam de Kooker, eating a huge slab of cake, came to ask how far away we were from the sea. He, among others, was worried about seasickness and was wondering when to take his tablets.

'Actually, we're almost there,' I said. 'It's reasonably calm, but if you're worried, take your tablets now.'

The northwest wind seemed to pick up a little and the rowers had to work hard not to drift south too much. We were now approaching the 'Queen's Channel' route out of the estuary and, while we knew we would have more traffic, we also knew we would have more water beneath us. Our plan was to travel a few yards south of the marked channel to keep away from the big ships. However, the channel is very narrow, and Roger Martell, skipper of Lecca Lecca, called on the radio a couple of times to say that a huge ship seemed to be coming right at them. While these ships did indeed pass quite close, I knew we were safe, as we were only in four metres of water, where no big ship would venture.

Jon Travers and Carl Van Katwyk were on duty in Tristan at that point. Jon was helming and, to preserve our night sight, he dimmed all the instruments to the point where you could hardly read them. He knew that as the darkness grew, so the instruments would appear brighter again. It was vital that those on watch could see any lights around us, and glare inside the boat would hamper this. The navigation lights went on outside and all cabin lights were extinguished. The most prominent light sources inside Tristan were now the faint green glow of the radar screen speckled with the echoes of the many ships using the busy Thames estuary and the soft glow of the red light illuminating the ship's compass. We kept a track of the nearest radar contacts, knowing that while we needn't worry about most of them, as they would keep to well-defined channels, we still had to be wary of fishing boats.

The rowers had switched on their solitary white light on the top of the 6ft mast at the front of the boat. I was pleased that it was bright enough - and high enough - to be seen. All around me I could see the red, green and white lights of the other support boats.

In the growing darkness and strengthening wind, we were all a bit on edge. The Rib had to keep shepherding the rowers north and there were a few cross words between the rowers and the Rib crew, as the former did not seem to grasp how shallow the water was getting just outside the channel.

The tide turned again and, as we approached the turning point that would take us south past North Foreland and out of the estuary, the wind picked up a little more. Although it would soon be behind them, the wind over tide made the sea short and choppy. The rowers were regularly getting a soaking.

By now it was pitch dark and the expected full moon had not yet risen. This was a low time for many of the rowers as tiredness, seasickness and nerves all took their toll. Thankfully, we knew this darkness would not last long as, even though the rising moon struggled to provide any light through the thick cloud cover, being early June, the sun would soon appear.

The peep, peep, peep from the chart plotter signalled it was time for a course change and Jon pushed the track button on the autopilot to accept the new course. He radioed the other vessels to let them know he what he was doing and confirmed his new heading. Our course now would take us through the infamous Goodwin Sands. To go around this series of sand banks would have added several miles to our journey and we were confident that, with reasonably good weather and all our navigation equipment, we should be able to safely negotiate this ships' graveyard. The exact number of vessels to have foundered here is unknown but is thought to be more than 2,000. When ships sink here the sands swallow them forever. The sands are 11 miles long and 6 miles wide and, while the navigable channel can shift, it is at least well marked.

Haddi's head appeared from around the side cabin door.

Good to go

'Are you coming to bed or not?' he said in a petulant voice, but smiling.

'Won't be long, darling,' I said, and the off-duty rowers around us fell about laughing. This had become a long-standing joke since the Amsterdam row. Haddi looks after everyone on board and I know, because he is a good mate and because he promised Ros that he would, he particularly looks out for me. Originally Haddi had asked the same question on the Amsterdam row because he was annoyed that I wasn't trying to get enough rest. He had said those words without really thinking and they had become part of our going-off-watch ritual.

The wind-over-tide conditions, together with the stress of navigating the dangerous Goodwins, started to make the mood more sombre. The sea was short, and the rowers struggled to keep a rhythm, often having to stop and wait for the rower in stroke position to get them all back into order. Every time they caught a crab (missed a stroke), the force of the water hitting the back of the oar blade would transfer directly and painfully through the carbon fibre oars to their already aching shoulders. The rower in bow position was regularly taking a soaking as the pointed stem of the rowing boat drove through, rather than over, the short chop.

At four o'clock in the morning, having tossed and turned for four hours, listening to the constant whirring of the autopilot and the splosh splosh of the sea passing the hull, I got out of my berth and whispered to Haddi in the opposite bunk: 'Time to get up, darling.'

'Thank heavens for that,' Haddi moaned in reply. Smiling, he said: 'I'm fed up with listening to the whirring of that autopilot and then having those inconsiderate rowers thumping over the deck every hour.'

The night had grown quite chilly. Karl had already poured tea for us, and I shivered as I drank mine, and Jon briefed me on the past four hours. It was already getting light. We had negotiated the Goodwins and were now quite close to South Foreland. Another major challenge completed successfully, and we were still within a mile of where the plan suggested we should have been. Jon and Karl retired to the still-warm bunks Haddi and I had just vacated, for their next four hours off watch.

During our journey down the Thames we had reported regularly to the Port of London Authorities to give them our position. Once we had left the estuary and rounded North Foreland, we made contact with the Dover Coastguard. We had spoken with the coastguard months earlier and I had called them the day before the start to let them know that things looked good for the off. Dover requested that we contact them every hour to report position, speed and course, so that they could include this information in their hourly navigation warnings to shipping. We knew they were keeping tabs on us as, during our third report, I had said: 'Speed about five knots,' and quick as flash the coastguard quipped: 'Five-and-a-half knots, actually'.

Our planned route took us across the very busy entrance to the Port of Dover and we had to stay at least a mile off the harbour entrance while making our crossing of the approach lanes. With careful radar control and the help of the coastguard, we crossed the entrance well away from all shipping and with no fuss. By now it was 6 o'clock and spirits lifted as the light grew stronger. We had completed 17 crew changes.

We received a message of support from the Dover coastguard to say that they were impressed with what the lads were trying to do and that they were very pleased with the professional approach to safety and planning. The coastguard promised to do a whip-round among their watch and said they would mention us to the local radio station. True to their word, there was a cheque from them waiting for me when I arrived home, with a charming letter which started with the wonderful line: 'We were delighted to have the pleasure of your company for a few hours...'

For some time after the row, we received a number of donations from people living around Dover and we guess these all came from the challenge having been mentioned on the local radio station.

Now we started the long pull west as, according to the French authorities, we had to go past the western end of the traffic separation scheme before we could turn south and cross the channel. The weather forecast suggested we should have very light north winds; in fact we had a strengthening westerly and rowing into it was becoming increasingly frustrating.

By the 24-hour mark, the rowers were feeling the effects of sleep deprivation. Some complained of the cold, others were suffering headaches and complaining of being 'spacey' and most were simply desperate to close their eyes and sleep. Now we were punching wind and tide and the rowers felt that they were not making any progress. In reality, the plan took the tide into consideration and despite the conditions, we were bang on target.

The rowers and crew knew that if they could turn south and cross the French shipping lanes, our course would be shortened by as much as two hours. Jason Hobbs, a crew member aboard Lecca Lecca, reacting to the comments voiced by the rowers, radioed to say he was unhappy to carry on west and wanted permission to turn south. I was slightly surprised that he was asking this, but then realised that because he had joined the Lecca Lecca crew quite late in the project, he had missed some of the explanations about the route and the agreed decision-making process. In fact I cursed myself because I should have made sure his training was complete.

I radioed back and explained that as we were within a mile of our planned position for that time and unless there was a good safety reason for going south, we would have to hold our course. Even if I altered course on grounds of safety, without the explicit authority of the French, we could be in serious trouble.

As soon as I passed this message I realised it was likely to dampen the spirits of the rowers further. While I regretted having to deny the request, I knew I really didn't have any option. I had spent so many hours wrestling with this problem before the start and it had also exasperated many of the committee members who, like me, struggled with the unfairness and poor reasoning of the French authority's decision not to allow us to cross.

I realised that the rowers and most of the crew on board Lecca Lecca were well aware of the French Admiral's decision to deny us permission to cross, but perhaps they also realised Jason was not aware of the history of this decision. This got me thinking – perhaps the same was true about the French. Perhaps the French Admiral's decision about this insignificant rowing team might not have registered with the lower echelon of the French coastguard. It also struck me that the French coastguard who deal with real shipping movements and problems each day might listen to a request for passage on grounds of safety and good seamanship. I called the Dover Coastguard and explained about the Admiral's decision and about the wind and the difficulty we were having with our present course. I asked Dover if they could possibly speak to the French on our behalf. Fifteen minutes later Dover Coastguard came back with the news that the French had accepted their British counterpart's recommendation to allow us to cross. The news immediately provided a boost to morale and we shaped a course to turn south.

Our original plan had taken account of the additional miles we'd have to cover to go around the end of the shipping lane. This plan also allowed us some leeway with regard the time we could arrive at the mouth of the Seine. We were now in the odd position of possibly saving two hours, which could mean we would arrive at the mouth of the Seine very early. This didn't really matter; it just meant the rowers would row against the last of the ebbing tide.

For a while after we changed course, the morale of the whole team lifted. Although the rowing was a little easier, the sea was still choppy. We crossed the shipping lanes and saw only one ship, and that passed about five miles away from us. Dover warned us that they would probably lose contact with us as we approached French waters and they asked us to establish contact with Cap Gris Nez, the French Coastguard for the area. We could not raise them. We tried on and off for more than an hour and eventually, having crossed the separation zone completely, we gave up trying.

Water had been carefully conserved on all the guard boats, as none of them were normally able to carry more than 150 gallons. We had not planned to be able to refill at any point, as the pilot books suggested it would be difficult to find anywhere in the Seine. This meant that without making other provisions, each person on the team would have about three gallons per day for drinking and washing. On Lecca Lecca this was further reduced as the toilets on board flushed with fresh water rather than seawater.

The three guard boats each had a different strategy for providing more water. Buz strapped two huge 45-gallon drums onto the foredeck of Access Challenger. Tristan is equipped with a water maker and I planned to run this on the second day once we were in the Channel.

Roger Martel in Lecca Lecca came up with one of his famously madcap schemes and planned to fill his two inflatable donuts, (the sort of thing you see being towed behind speed boats in the Med, filled with screaming holidaymakers) and strap them onto his foredeck. During the planning meetings there was a lot of laughter generated by Roger's plan and I admit to being the ringleader of this derision. Roger had filled the donuts in London and, amazingly, his plan worked perfectly.

My idea to run the water maker fell apart when the generator overheated and blew its capacitor. Roger was quite entitled to the last laugh. It wasn't long before the radio waves were full of quips from the other guard boats. Thankfully, Tristan is equipped with a piece of kit called an inverter, which changes the 12 volts produced by the engines into 240 volts. The inverter doesn't produce enough power to run hungry equipment like water makers, but it will boil a small kettle so our tea supply was not interrupted.

Plans to conserve water included restricting each person to one short shower per day and, on board Lecca Lecca, Roger had worked out a way of reducing the use of fresh water through his toilets. During the river passages, when there was no swell to make the practice unsafe, anyone wanting a pee on board Lecca Lecca was required to go with a 'toilet mate' to pee off the bathing platform. This system meant that the 'mate' held onto the boat with one hand while grasping the back of the shirt of the person who was making use of the outside loo. This practice provided a wealth of material to boost the already rich pickings for our on-board comedians. I have to say that my best memories of the trip are all about laughter; even during the tough times, laughter was never far away.

While still in range of the British cellphone system, I made contact with David Farrimond, our anchorman in Guernsey. I told him about the problem with the generator. He said: 'Give me the details of the part and I will see what I can do.'

As the sun started to set, the wind increased noticeably, and with the wind on our starboard beam, all the guard boats began rocking and pitching. None of the guard boats were designed to travel at this low speed and the dynamics of the hulls, which would normally provide some stability, could not come into play.

Slowly, the wind increased until by about 11 pm we were in a force five. I cursed all weather forecasters – none of them had predicted this. Things are always worse in the dark, and it was very true that night, that the darkest hour was the hour before dawn. The rowers were taking a battering when they were rowing and they were becoming sick when they were meant to be resting. On board the guard boats, everyone had to hold on and brace all the time. The rowers were completely unable to rest, and many of them were violently ill. Unusually for me, I was not feeling even the slightest twinge of seasickness, and I marvelled that I could look at all those around me, and at the wildly moving boats near us, without feeling even the slightest bit ill. I could even navigate and read with no problem. I guess it must have been the adrenalin.

Matt Harradine, however, who had been dreading seasickness, was particularly ill and his fellow team members were worried that he was becoming dehydrated. Doctor Gee was ferried over in the Rib to assess him and see what he could do. He injected some magic potion and an hour later Matt was so much better he was laughing again. Somewhat bizarrely, he was now laughing at other people being sick.

Good to go

On board Tristan and Lecca Lecca, at least one of the eight rowers based on each boat would be on a long rest at any one time. This was meant to be a five-hour break and, as such, the rower was encouraged to try to sleep as much as possible. On Tristan the long rest rower usually chose the aft cabin, which has a double bed, and although it is noisier than the forward cabin, there is less motion. Often there would be two or three rowers trying to get some rest in the aft cabin, and the 'on watch' rowers were careful to move around the cabin quietly, using torch light so as not to disturb them.

Relentlessly, the crew changes took place on the hour every hour. In the darkness and with the increased swell, the changeovers became more and more difficult. Added to this, the rowers were now very tired and their mental stamina was being tested. It was now over 30 hours since the start, which meant we had completed 30 crew changes. Many of the rowers hadn't slept since we left London.

I was becoming concerned about the part of the changeover where the rowers transferred from the Rib to the guard boats. With the two boats rolling out of sync, one second the hulls were level, the next the Rib could be six feet above or below. The rowers had to time their leap precisely. I felt, especially in such darkness, this was just too dangerous. The guard boat skippers discussed the situation over the radio and we agreed that, until the wind abated, the transfers would be carried out while running down wind. To accomplish this, both the guard boat and the Rib had to turn 90 degrees to our intended course and run down the waves together. That way, most of the movement was pitching rather than rolling.

This worked well, but it meant that, as soon as the transfer had been made, the boat crews had to work hard to get back on course. In the dark, with the boats tossing endlessly, it was difficult to keep tabs on the rowing boat and the other support boats, and to make sure we were not running into other shipping.

At approximately 10.00 pm (BST) the rudder came off again. The team struggled in the dark and with the violent pitching to get it back on. Shortly after this, the rowing boat ploughed into a submerged object. We never did find out what it was, but it must have been something pretty massive, as it stopped the boat completely. The Rib driver drew alongside to inspect the damage and it was clear that a part of the bow had been stoved in and the first watertight section had been breached. Among the crew, we had a wealth of boat-building experience and there was general agreement that while the boat would be heavier, it was not in danger of sinking. Some of the crew suggested we try to repair the bow immediately, but I felt we would do better to wait for daylight. I also reckoned it would be far easier to carry out the repair in the river which, by now, was only about 10 miles away. The other factor was that if we spent more time at sea, we might miss the first of the flood tide that was so essential to get us up the daylight-only section of the Seine. The rowers started off again but were having real problems steering. The damage to the bow had produced a flap of ply that was acting as a bow rudder, and this, combined with the proper rudder coming off again, made it hard to keep on track. Buz White in Access Challenger, acting as lead boat, was becoming frustrated as he tried in vain to keep the rowers on course.

It was clear now that a few of the rowers and one or two of the guard boat crew were starting to contemplate failure. A few of the team were definitely ready to give up. I thought about the alternatives, but we were so close to the French shore, surely we wouldn't give up now? To add to the difficulties, the tide was now flowing strongly to the east and for an hour-and-a-half we didn't make any progress. Interestingly, had we not turned south early we would have had the wind a little more on our stern and we would not be fighting to gain ground to the west. On balance, though, the early turn saved us two hours and I kept this in mind as I tried to lift the team's spirits. I just kept assuring everyone that we were very much on target, which we were, and that things would seem much better in an hour or so, when dawn arrived. I am not sure anyone believed me and at that moment I felt quite useless as a project leader.

Colin's resolve, however, hadn't wavered one inch. Originally, he had wanted to be a roving rower, visiting and rowing with each rowing crew in turn. He wanted to do this because on previous rows, the crew that was without Colin's constant influence and motivation always felt a little left out. Thankfully, at about 3 am there was a noticeable decrease in the wind and the sea started to calm. As day broke, we crossed the approach lanes to Le Havre and made our way towards the entrance to the Seine.

It turned out that the two hours we saved by not going around the end of the sea lanes had been lost again through a combination of the row boat being damaged and by the rowers fighting the tide more than they would have had we not turned early.[8] But incredibly, overall, after 40 hours and 200 miles, we were within an hour of our planned schedule. We had now completed 40 crew changes, and I knew these would be a lot easier as soon as we reached the flat water of the river.

---

[8] For illustrations of planned route and actual course taken, please see appendix 2 & 3.

Chapter ten – It's not over yet

08:30 BST Saturday 5th June at the mouth of the Seine.

***

Buz's calm voice came over the radio: 'Tristan, Tristan – Access.'

'Go ahead, Buz,' I said.

'We are aground!' Buz said.

As he relayed this horrifying message, we too ground to a halt and I quickly put the engine into neutral. Only then did our depth alarm sound. Lecca Lecca joined in the radio traffic to say they too had touched. Buz called again to say he was floating clear and that he was already in deeper water.

I called to the Rib to tow me out, but as they made their way over to us, we re-floated and I nudged Tristan ahead on one engine. I knew we were on a rising tide and also knew that the bottom in this area was sand, so I was pretty sure that we would not have done any damage. All the crews scrutinised the charts to try to find our error, but the charts all showed a minimum depth of 3 metres in this area. I made a mental note to line up all marine cartographers next to all forecasters for the firing squad. To be reasonable, sand banks do continually shift and it is impossible to be certain of depths in such areas.

Within half an hour of our grounding incident, we had arrived at the first of the buoys marking the Seine estuary. I checked the tide flow and found we had half a knot with us. We had arrived smack on time, literally within minutes of our planned arrival time. This meant we would benefit from the whole of the flood tide. Within 20 minutes, the tide flow had grown to one-and-a-half knots.

177

Complying with instructions, I made contact with the Rouen port control to report our arrival. They were fairly uninterested and asked us to report again just before we arrived within the port area, which was still 60 miles away. The controller warned us sternly to keep out of the way of commercial traffic. We were proceeding just to the north of the buoyed channel and there was a constant stream of huge ships making their way up with the flood tide, on the south side of the channel. The channel is narrow and the ships seemed quite close. Jason on Lecca Lecca was not convinced that we were following the correct approach and called me on the radio.

'Rob, I think we should be on the other side of the river - surely you always keep to the right hand side?'

'No,' I said. 'We must stay on this side until we get past port buoy number 32 and then cross at right angles to the other side.'

Minutes later, Jason was back on the radio again.

'I really think we should be on the other side,' he said. 'I think we should cross now.'

I was tired, concentrating like mad, and trying to work out a good place to begin the repair to the rowing boat. I felt an enormous sense of frustration at being questioned over this matter and really wanted to say: 'If you had read the passage plan properly and the same three pilot books I read months ago, it would be quite clear,' but I knew that would be unnecessarily pompous and confrontational.

Even so, I nearly blew my top when he made this request yet again. 'Our instructions are clear,' I said in as loud and forceful manner I could manage. 'You will *not* cross the channel and you *will* stay on your course until I signal otherwise.' Poor old Jason got the message and simply radioed back 'received'. I was angry that I had broken my own rule of not shouting commands. He was right to question me and I perhaps should have spent more time explaining how it was that the normal rules of river navigation didn't apply for this stretch of the Seine. I suppose too, Jason might have felt justified in questioning the passage plan, considering we had gone aground earlier!

The flood tide was now running at five knots and we were managing 10 knots over the ground. At this speed, we would have to act fast once we had spotted a stretch of river where we could do the repair.

Buz had worked out that there was a straight, wide stretch of the river about half-a-mile ahead, with sufficient depth for us to drift out of the way of other river traffic. Now the planning really paid off. Buz had the glue, screws, grinder and plywood ready.

The Rib shepherded the rowing boat over to the correct position. The rowers leapt out of the rowing boat into it. Buz cut his engines, as we felt that using them during this manoeuvre might invalidate the record attempt. The bow of the rowing boat was lifted onto the side of Access Challenger and, like a team of surgeons, our various boat builders set to work at a furious pace. First they emptied the water from the flooded compartment.

Someone would work out later that the water weighed about 100 kilos. Then, in little more than five minutes they had smoothed off the damaged ply, made two patches, glued and screwed the repair and bandaged the whole thing in duct tape for good measure.

There was one hairy moment as the wake from a huge tanker swung the rowing boat round and threatened to pull it off the side off Access Challenger. With the massive muscle power of the team and copious swearing, they managed to hang on to the boat. Moments later they were able to slip the bow back into the water and the rowers were off again. The repair had been achieved while drifting at five knots, so during those 10 minutes, we had travelled over half-a-mile up river.

It's not over yet

Having arrived at the mouth of the river exactly on schedule, I was fairly confident that this put us at least six hours ahead of the record, but I still resisted being this specific when giving out information about our progress. We had very little knowledge of the precise details of previous attempts, and more importantly, I didn't know what conditions higher up the river might do to this supposed lead. I chose still just to announce that we were on schedule and that we were on target to break the record 'by a good margin'. I couldn't help feeling a mounting sense of excitement, though, as to get this far, bang on schedule, was in itself a massive achievement. Sleep was impossible, but I made a point of going off duty and lying in my bunk.

Previous rows had impressed upon us just how important the guard boat crew was in looking after the rowers and lifting their spirits. No one was more aware of this than Haddi.

Unlike many of the boat crew, Haddi has not spent his life on the water and his interest in boating had come only in the last couple of years. He was quite worried about being seasick - not so much because of the discomfort, but because he was worried that he wouldn't be able to do his duty and look after the rowers. He constantly fiddled with his sea bands during his watches to ensure they were precisely in the right position. It wasn't to be until we had tied up in Paris that he turned to me and asked whether I thought it would be safe to take them off.

Haddi and Karl were always there to greet the rowers coming off duty and to ensure they transferred safely from the Rib. They would always have the kettle on, and a hot cup of tea was ready within moments of the chaps coming back on board. This took some doing during the passage across the channel, with the boat pitching and rolling constantly. Haddi has an irrepressible sense of humour. No-one on board Tristan could fail to be impressed that he could busy himself in the depths of the galley while being thrown all over the place, before appearing with more fresh tea and a hilarious comment.

At one point he emerged from the galley, tea in hand and with a thick rubber band around his head clamping a mobile phone painfully to his ear.

'What the hell are you up to, Haddi?' I asked.

'My daughter gave this to me before we left,' he said. 'Said it was a hands-free kit.'

It was a relief to be in the flat water of the river and most of us grabbed the opportunity to have a wash and tidy things up a bit. The crew on board Tristan had been keen to keep things fairly tidy all along, as a tidy ship is good for morale.

Haddi went to put the kettle on for the 100th time.

'Water's not working,' he said. 'Pump must have gone.'

With careful use of the water - we still had over half a tank – we knew we hadn't run out.

'I'll pull the floor up and swap pumps,' Haddi said. The film crew were on board Tristan at this point and were busy documenting this latest instalment of Tristan's water drama.

'Hell – this is going to give the Lecca Lecca boys a laugh,' I said. Haddi moved all the saloon seating and pulled up the flooring panels, exposing the port engine. Tucked outboard of the engine were the two water pumps and switching system. Haddi switched over the pumps and we tried the galley tap again.

'Nothing,' Haddi said.

We fiddled around with the pipes and wiring for five minutes but couldn't get anything to run. Haddi used to work for the firm that made Tristan and actually fits all the water system to all the new boats so is pretty knowledgeable. Jon Travers, Tristan's other watch leader and probably the best all-round engineer amongst us, was off watch.

It's not over yet

'Jon's asleep at the moment; maybe we should wait for him to come on duty,' I suggested.

At this, Jon popped his head out from the side cabin.

'It's all right; I'm not asleep – too damn smooth to sleep!'

Jon went to the galley tap, turned it on and water gushed out.

'Fixed it,' he said and without another word he disappeared back into the side cabin.

Haddi was seething: 'All this caught on film – I hope no one at work gets to see it.' We never did find out exactly what caused the problem; our best guess was an air lock, caused by a leaky water filter.

It was getting warmer, the sun was shining and we were now steering Tristan from the flybridge. It was easy to check our progress as there are kilometre markings on the riverbank. We were also making use of a wonderful publication, the Navicart, which documented every feature of the Seine.

Another sure sign that things were looking up was the never-ending flow of rowers making meals in the galley. Rowing is a tremendous calorie burner and they were doing their best, in the short rest periods, to replace as many calories as they could. A favourite meal would be a huge portion of reconstituted dry mashed potato with a can or two of baked beans mixed in, followed by a couple of Kit Kats or half a packet of Jaffa Cakes. The rowers were eating perhaps as many as seven or eight meals a day, with snacks on top. Then, throughout their rest hour, they would drink, slowly sipping perhaps as much as one-and-a-half or two litres of liquid. Colin had impressed upon his team that the secret of re-hydrating is not to dehydrate in the first place, and to drink before you exercise.

My phone rang; it was Tony Cullington, reporting that he had all the vignettes (licences) for all the boats for the

Seine and saying that he had a capacitor for me. David Farrimond had found one in Guernsey and managed to get it shipped to Carteret, where Tony's father, Geoff, had picked it up and driven to meet Tony. We arranged to rendezvous with Tony a few miles upriver, where they had found a quay where one of the guard boats could stop for a minute or two. Having the generator working again was certainly a boost, but we couldn't use the water maker in the river, so Tristan's water reserves were still a problem.

During one of the early shifts up the tidal section of the Seine, I was off duty and was looking at the difference flat water made to the rowers' progress. Their smooth strokes were in such contrast to the often erratic, jarring motion caused by the frustratingly difficult conditions of the previous night. The lads were really going for it now and I watched with a little concern as Adek in stroke position grimaced with the effort of each pull of the oars. He was the oldest member of the rowing team and his son, who was also rowing, was the youngest. The sort of pace these guys were managing to keep up for an hour your average Joe wouldn't manage for more than a few minutes.

When the crew changed over, I helped Adek on board and he was covered in sweat and looked exhausted.

'Adek,' I said, 'Blimey mate you were going for it – there's another 200 miles to go yet: shouldn't you be pacing yourself a bit?'

He gave me the sort of exasperated half-smile that perhaps a wise old granddad might give his tiresome grandson.

Patting me heavily on the back he said: 'Look, Rob, you take care of the navigation and we'll look after the rowing – we've got a world record to get.'

We had started the row on what I had estimated to be the last possible day on that tidal cycle. I reckoned this was the last day in which we would have enough light to safely complete the daylight only section of the Seine. The lads now had to keep a steady pace and we had to hope for no other incidents to slow or stop us until we were past Rouen, which was about 60 miles upriver.

A few hours after entering the Seine, Gary Seabrook was on duty in the Rib and he called on the radio to say he was getting low on diesel. We weren't sure of the range of the Rib so we had made provision for an 'in-flight' refuelling system. We called for him to come alongside Tristan and to attach the bow rope just as they had been doing during crew changes. Haddi then lifted a couple of floor panels, exposing the fuel transfer pump usually used to transfer diesel from between Tristan's two 250-gallon fuel tanks. Before we had left, Haddi had rigged a two-way valve with a length of hose long enough to exit Tristan through the cabin window and overboard to the Rib. With this system we refuelled the Rib in a couple of minutes from Tristan's ample reserve, without stopping. The boys in the Rib were really impressed and Haddi felt he had now regained his street cred, which had taken a bit of a knock over the water pump incident.

Spirits were really high and the rowing pace was such that I had every confidence we would pass Rouen within the required time. We had strict instructions to keep right into the left bank (the left bank is the right bank as you go up river – confusing for the uninitiated, I know) and not to cut corners. The Rib drivers constantly shepherded the rowers, but one set of rowers in particular kept trying to straighten out the river. It wiggles and bends all the way to Paris and it is easy to see why the daylight-only rule exists. By late afternoon we had negotiated France's fifth-largest port and had easily passed the upper limit of the daylight-only section. With this latest obstacle safely behind us, we looked forward to reaching the first lock.

Although we had managed to keep the flood with us for nearly 10 hours, the tide had now turned and our speed over the ground gradually fell to about 4 knots. At 9.30

pm I radioed the first lock at Amfreville to let them know we were approaching. Tony Cullington was waiting there and intercepted the radio traffic to let us know everything was ready and that the keeper had the gates open for us.

We had worked out, in minute detail, the procedure for entering the locks. Locks were the most dangerous part of the river and we were determined to make them as safe as possible. Each guard boat skipper had a printed copy of the procedure, which we had reduced to a few lines to make it as simple as possible. I reached for my copy and checked we were all in the right position. I didn't have to say anything and the team went through the procedure as if they had been doing it all their lives. Very few instructions were needed and there were certainly no raised voices.

At 10.00 pm, we passed through the lock gates. We were about one hour behind my estimated timing, but I wasn't worried, as we were still on to break the record by seven hours if everything else went to plan. The lock was lit by sodium floodlights and was absolutely massive. All four support boats and the rowing boat took up only one small section of one side of the lock.

Tony had found a water hose and I decided to take a few minutes to top up Tristan's fast-depleting tanks. With the lock cycle complete, the other boats set off into the darkness and we arranged to catch up with them in 10 or 15 minutes time. Having decided to stop for water I had a niggling feeling that I was making a mistake. After all, I was the one constantly telling everyone not do anything that wasn't in the plan. We didn't completely fill the tanks, as it was taking too long and I didn't want to be too far away from the others. We left the lock and motored into complete darkness. The moon hadn't yet risen and there were no features on the banks to be seen. To add to the difficulty, a mist had developed and eerie shapes developed around us. It was impossible to tell what they were. I remained on the flybridge and John Travers, who was officially off watch, volunteered to use the radar to navigate us during this difficult time. John relayed instructions via the intercom.

'You need to take the second branch on the right,' he said.

I strained to make out the turnings in the gloom and was starting to get anxious that we wouldn't be able to go fast enough in the dark to catch up with the others. I took what I thought was the second turning, but immediately questioned myself. It looked too narrow and appeared to be a cul de sac. I spun Tristan in her own length and stopped. I had resisted using the searchlight, as it would ruin my night vision but now switched it on, as I accepted we needed more guidance, even if it meant we had to be slower. To my right, on what seemed to be the end of an island, there was a sign which clearly indicated the direction of the main channel. I had taken the turn too early. Desperate to catch up, stupidly I gunned Tristan's engines and in a few yards, we were probably travelling at five knots. Tristan's bow rode up as she ploughed into a mud bank and came to an abrupt halt. I had forgotten that downstream of most islands there is a build up of silt – I hadn't allowed enough room down river of the sign. How could I have managed this? I had spent enough years fishing in the Thames to know the dangers and vagaries of rivers.

I put Tristan gently into reverse, but she remained glued to the mud. I increased the revs, churning up the muddy bottom; still she didn't move an inch. I called Buz and asked him to turn round to tow me out. Oh crap! - I had gone aground twice in 24 hours.

I shouted for everyone to get on deck as quickly as possible. The lads tumbled through the aft door, some still with sandwiches in their hands and most in varying states of undress.

I didn't want to give up trying to get off on our own and assembled all who were on board on the aft deck. Even with the weight of all 10 rowers and crew right aft, she wouldn't move.

Think, Rob, think!

I remembered all those stories I had read about old men of war going aground or getting stuck on uncharted reefs. They used to throw off all their cannons, their anchors, water and any other heavy material. I considered pumping out the water we had just taken on, but that would have taken ages. Chucking our 45-kilogram anchor overboard would be a puny gesture.

Then it came to me.

We lowered Tristan's small dinghy into the water and I urged all 10 lads to squeeze into it. There wasn't room for them to sit; they all had to stand upright, packed as tight as sardines, to get in the tiny craft. Now that we had got rid of the weight of all the people on board I gunned both engines again and, slowly at first, Tristan started to slip backwards. We were free!

I contacted Buz again to let him know the good news.

'Thank heavens for that,' he said. 'I thought navigation last night was difficult – this is a nightmare.'

Later, Buz, a member of the Guernsey lifeboat crew, said that it had been the most difficult night of navigation in his career.

I know now I should not have stopped for water. It was my first and, I hoped, last, bad error of judgement. I had been urging everyone else to keep to the plan, but had been vain enough to think the rule didn't apply to me.

We set off to catch up with the other boats but proceeded at a much slower pace. The mist had slowed them, so it only took about 20 minutes before we spotted their lights. During that time the radio waves were busy with communication between all the boats and it was obvious just how brilliantly all the vessels were working together. Listening to the calm instructions and observations, I was struck by the sheer professionalism and determination of the team. It was so difficult for the rowers, as not only was it pitch black and misty, but the rower responsible for steering was facing backwards! The Rib drivers, in conjunction with Buz, coached and guided the rowing boat, and it is testament to their skill that they made it through the small hours without a hitch. I was mighty happy to rejoin the flotilla, as navigation was far easier and safer as a group.

For the first time I allowed myself to believe that we really could smash this record. As soon as I had this thought I castigated myself – I must not allow the tiniest bit of complacency to creep in – anywhere.

Now that we were in the non-tidal section of the Seine, the river was very shallow. We had set our depth alarm to three metres and it was constantly sounding. The good news was that the background current was much less than we had allowed for and was actually less than a knot. Our plan had allowed for one of two knots so, every hour, we should be gaining 1.5 miles.

At a little after 2 am we reached the second lock and the cycle went quickly and smoothly. Shortly after exiting, we carried out our 60th crew change.

Dawn broke, and those of us on watch were rewarded not only with the relief of easier navigation but also with a spectacular display of nature's beauty. A thin, wispy mist clung to the river and the hillsides. The water was mirror-calm. As the sunlight strengthened, the mist took on a thousand shades of orange and pink and the rowers' oars made perfect swirling patterns that trailed their boat. The crew on board Tristan were quiet – as though forced into an ecclesiastical silence by the stillness of all around. It was all such a contrast to the man-made squalor, noise and bustle of the Thames.

It's not over yet

Most of us had hardly slept since Wednesday night in St Katherine's Dock. I had forced myself to lie in my bunk when off watch, but still I just could not sleep. I am sure I had too much adrenalin in my system for it to shut down for more than a few minutes. I had a strange buzzing in my head most of the time, my eyes felt gritty and I was exhausted. I was very conscious that I was not thinking as quickly or as clearly as normal. The antics of the previous night proved that much. Surely though, what I was feeling was nothing compared to what the rowers were going through. At the same time, however, I was so excited I had constant butterflies in my stomach. It was odd, but time was flying, and it was hard to believe we had already been going nearly three days. I remember resolving to think twice and do once, and went on to urge the rest of the team to do the same.

It didn't take much for the rowers and boat crews to start laughing and now that a respectable period of time had elapsed, the team comedians started making fun of our exploits in the small hours of the previous night.

'Cross ply or radials, Rob?' came the message from Jo Paul on board Lecca Lecca. Jo has perhaps the most irrepressible humour of all the rowers.

'What are you talking about?' I said.

'For Tristan - What tyres are you planning for Tristan, now you seem to prefer land to water?' he joked. The jokes went on and on. I was just so pleased we could now laugh about it and, frankly, I deserved all the ribbing I was to receive.

We reached the third lock at Mericourt at seven on the Sunday morning. Tony and Jane Cullington were there to greet us. Not only did they have the lock keeper ready and primed for a fast cycle, but also they supplied us with fresh croissants and baguettes. We still had three more locks and 75 miles to go.

189

It was obvious by now that unless we did something really stupid, the rowers would smash the record.

It was impressive, therefore, that if anything, the rowers were stepping up the pace. By this stage, previous teams had been falling apart and we had heard that some rowers had even refused to do their sessions.

We did have the odd moan from a couple of rowers that others were not rowing as fast, but overall the team spirit was magnificent. Colin stamped on the 'We are quicker than them' stuff very firmly, reminding everyone that there was only one team. Looking back, it was a bit rich, anyway, as the rowers who were complaining were the same characters who, two nights previously, had been contemplating giving up.

Above: Early Sunday morning, Jon on Tristan lights the way.

Below: the film crew recording a crew change

Early Sunday morning on the Seine

At 1.00 pm on Sunday: arriving at Andresey lock

The day began to get very hot. Colin had been having a problem with inflammation of the eyelids and was in constant discomfort. It was probably caused by the continual soaking in sea spray for several days. Buckets of sweat were now adding to his problems. The bright sunshine increased his discomfort but he searched out an old wide-brimmed hat and sunglasses and carried on rowing.

When the rowers changed over, the returning crews headed straight for the power drinks. They were desperate to replace the litres of fluid and the salt they had lost in the past hour.

A pungent stench of sweaty rubber was ever present inside Tristan now. The cause was the neoprene slip-on boots the rowers wore, and which were in desperate need of a good wash. I had become aware of this problem on the last row, when the acrid smell had hung around for weeks.

This time, I had covered all the carpets with see through plastic 'carpet saver'. This stuff had spikes on one side so that it was meant to stay in place. The trouble was, it was forever being flipped over by the constant movement through the cabins and, if you were walking around barefoot, it was a painful experience.

Exhausted, Colin (left) and Lloyd, rest their eyes and enjoy one of the hundreds of cups of tea made by crew member "Kettle-on" (AKA Dave Hadlington).

The rowers did everything they could to reduce the chance of friction injuries. Many of them had seen poor old Mark Shepherd struggling to walk after the last row. A number of them walked around the saloon starkers to allow fresh air to get everywhere and others applied copious amounts of petroleum jelly to their "under carriage" to ease the problem. They didn't seem to feel the need to do this in private.

Haddi had put out a number of bowls and containers with various high-energy foods around the main cabin. I made the mistake of going for a fistful of peanuts, only to find them suspiciously sticking together. I lost my appetite for peanuts immediately and permanently.

Another smell that had been present for much of the time, at least whenever we were quite close to Access Challenger, was that of bacon cooking.

Buz is a great one for simplicity and he reckoned provisioning for his crew could mostly be achieved with three commodities: bacon, bread and cheese, and they existed almost exclusively on those foods. Typically it was bacon sandwiches for breakfast, cheese sandwiches for lunch and bacon and cheese sandwiches for dinner.

For the guard boat crews, apart from the tiredness, this period was really enjoyable. I cannot think of many better ways of spending a day than meandering slowly up a beautiful river with the sun shining. The ever-changing scenery ensures the river cruiser is never bored and in addition to the natural beauty of the Seine, there was a constant stream of man-made distractions and attractions.

On most of the upper sections of the river there is a speed limit that ensures the river traffic proceeds at a sedate pace, preserving the river banks and the sanity of those who live on house boats. However, every so often you come across a derestricted stretch that allows water-skiers, wake boarders and the like, to practise.

As Paris grew nearer, the level of human activity around us increased. At one point, the rowers and guard boats had to negotiate a regatta with about 20 sailing boats. Close to the city, we watched as a dancer practised his art on the towpath. We passed scores of houseboats, some in disrepair, hardly floating but most lovingly painted and bedecked with pot plants. Their occupants watched us go by; a few cheered us on and many clapped politely as we passed.

As we negotiated the last lock at Bourgival, the team was a little quieter. We had just 20 miles to go.

It was tempting now to get excited about the finish and, because everything was happening like clockwork, it would have been easy to let our minds wander and make a mistake or miss some vital detail. But going aground after Amfreville Lock was all the reminder I needed to keep focussed.

Despite Colin's constant calls to the team to be careful and hold their concentration I knew he too couldn't help the odd moment of reflection. At one point he slapped me on the back and said: 'You do realise you'll be entitled to change your name to "Le Platts" from now on?'

'My ancestors from Normandy changed their name from Le Platts to Platts when we invaded England with some chap called William[9],' I replied. 'I wouldn't mind changing it back again though,' I said, grinning.

To exhaustion was added apprehension. We were now so close – but victory was not yet ours. I think maybe Colin shared my apprehension and he got on the radio to speak to all the rowers and crews to add weight to my earlier warning that now we really had to concentrate, and ensure there were no slip-ups. We approached the last lock (Suresnes) and, as usual, our magnificent shore team

---

[9] Pure speculation based on some research completed by my father looking into our family history.

was there to greet us. Tony Cullington had been monitoring the radio traffic and couldn't believe the speed the rowers were still achieving. At this point, we were over 10 hours in front of the record.

Tony warned us that the lock keeper was really interested in this challenge, and was determined to do the fastest cycle possible. The gates were open waiting for us and the second the last guard boat was in, the huge doors swung shut. We had only just secured all the lines when the sluices were opened and it started to fill at an alarming rate. We had become a bit blasé about the procedure, but on this occasion the water came gushing through and tried to force the entire flotilla to the back of the huge lock basin. The rowers hung on to the Rib with all their might and I flinched as Tristan's dock lines groaned with the strain. In less than three minutes the flood subsided and the upper lock gates were being opened.

Now for the final stretch.

There were so many bridges. During the planning we had to check the height of all the bridges, as we needed at least 20 feet clearance to get the tallest guard boat through. This did not stop us worrying, as each successive bridge seemed to be getting lower and lower and we all held our breath and stared up as we negotiated each one.

Until that is, Jon Travers said: 'Right, that's it – I have had enough, that aerial is coming down!'

He nipped up the radar arch with a spanner between his teeth and lowered the VHF radio aerial to improve our air draught by a few feet.

Houses, warehouses and offices had slowly replaced the beautiful countryside and now the tall buildings of Paris were plainly in view.

We were fast approaching what would be the 78th and last crew changeover. Obviously, all the rowers wanted to be in the rowing boat to cross the line, but only five would have that privilege.

When the Jersey team had reached this point there had been a huge argument, which apparently almost ended in fisticuffs. We had learnt from this, and it had been understood from the start that even if there were only five minutes to go, a crew change would still happen as normal. This meant that a crew from Lecca Lecca would be rowing on the last leg.

The Eiffel Tower plainly in view – almost there.

I was sitting on the flybridge with Colin about 20 minutes before this last changeover and we received a call from Lecca Lecca.

'The lads on Lecca Lecca are all agreed. Mark (Colin's brother-in-law) wants Colin to take his place on the last crew changeover.'

Colin was stunned and immediately tears rolled down his face. Choking on his tears, Colin said to me: 'I can't speak.'

I radioed back: 'Message received, Colin will call you back on this.'

This was an amazing gesture by Mark and one that was very popular. Every one of the rowers wanted the rowing team leader to be in the boat at the finish. When Colin regained his composure he radioed back: 'Tell Mark I am overwhelmed by his offer but we have agreed a plan - it's been a good plan so far and we are sticking to it.'

We now had less than two miles to go and, all of a sudden there it was: the Eiffel tower. Now we were down to the last mile and the amount of river traffic had trebled. Memories of my last visit to the busy river in Paris came flooding back. I studied the traffic around me carefully, nervous of the sheer size and number of vessels.

We had dressed Tristan in bunting from stem to stern and all the lads on board gathered on the bow to cheer the rowers on the last leg. I knew there would be a sprint finish, but this was ridiculous. It was as though the last three days of non-stop rowing and sleep deprivation had been completely forgotten. Up to this point, we had been proceeding under one engine and swapping each hour. With this increase in pace I switched on both and we raced towards the centre of Paris at almost seven knots.

Then, we were approaching one of the last bridges before the finish and one of the enormous sightseeing vessels known as a bateau mouche, with a wedding party on board, suddenly left its mooring on our starboard side.

This huge craft managed to get in between the rowing boat and all the support boats.

We couldn't have this – all this way, all this work: we couldn't not be with the rowers at the finish.

We drew alongside the bateau mouche with Lecca Lecca behind. I could see that Roger was furious at this last minute intervention and he was standing, hands open, as if to say: 'What the hell is his game?'

I waved frantically at the old skipper on board the French boat, but I couldn't get his attention.

I had to get in front. I put both engines to full power and Tristan's 750 horsepower made her leap forward. The bow rose, almost toppling the lads standing at the front. They all cheered as they realised what I was trying to do. I sounded Tristan's horn with five long blasts[10]. We were now overtaking the wedding party and flying past the bride and groom, who were looking amused on the aft deck. As we passed the bow, I cut in and waved at the skipper to slow down. He had no choice, or he would have run us down.

Access Challenger, Lecca Lecca and the Rib took advantage and powered past. The flotilla was soon reunited for the last quarter-mile. We could see the Pont d'Helena clearly now, and draped over the down-river side of this elegant bridge was an enormous Guernsey flag. The Eiffel tower loomed over us.

Then we were through and over the line, all the ship's horns going non-stop, the crowds on the shore cheering and all the rowers making a racket with air drums. The crowds of people gathered on the river banks and on the bridge grew, as more people came to see what all the fuss was about.

Over all the noise, I just caught the radio traffic from Dr Gee confirming that we had pulverised the record by

---

[10] Five long blasts means, "I do not understand your intentions."

over 11 hours to finish in 79 hours 9 minutes 26 seconds. We had set a new World Record!

At the start we had three objectives: to be safe and bring everyone home in one piece, to break the world record and to raise money to fund an MS nurse. We had arrived bruised, battered and knackered, but in one piece. The record was ours, and we had raised £140,000. The island of Guernsey would now have an MS nurse.

When the Jersey team had established their time, they went on record as saying: 'If anyone thinks they can break that time, they are welcome to try.'

Now it was our turn to issue the same challenge.

The Rowers shortly after the finish (picture Mark Dravers)

Guard boat "Tristan" cheering the rowers (picture Mark Dravers)

The rowers carrying Charlie Trebilcock back up the steps of Pont d'Helena
(picture Mark Dravers)

Chapter eleven: One night in Paris

The guard boats pulled over to the right bank just above Pont d'Helena. By now, relatives and friends had made their way down to the bank hoping to greet the victorious rowers.

The boat crews swarmed ashore and, as if by magic (we had agreed no alcohol on any of the boats), cans of beer and bottles of champagne appeared.

One of the first people to greet us was Mark Dravers. Mark, who had flown me over to Paris a couple of weeks previously, this time had brought our anchorman, David Farrimond, and my mate Charlie Trebilcock. Charlie has MS and his disease had progressed to the point where he needed to use a wheelchair most of the time. Mark told us Charlie was still up on the bridge because there was a steep bank of marble steps preventing him from getting down to the riverside. Colin and a few of the rowers sprang into action and carried a beaming and laughing Charlie, still in his wheelchair, down the steps. This will always be an abiding memory for me. It summed up all that was good about Guernsey's community getting together to help fellow islanders defeat barriers.

Although none of us wanted to get back into the boats just yet, the day was marching on and it was getting dark. There was a reception with the Paris MS Society arranged for that evening but we had a few tasks left. We had to get the rowing boat out of the water and on to its trailer. Once that was achieved the guard boats had a short trip to the moorings, which had been reserved, right next to the Eiffel Tower. We only had time for a quick shower before we all marched off, trying to find the venue for this reception.

We were all so tired by this point that I don't think any of us were really thinking straight. For the first time in days my mind was telling me that I had to sleep.

One night in Paris

The representatives from the Paris MS Society were very welcoming but I think they probably thought we were all barking mad. But the Parisians, like Guernsey folk don't need much of an excuse and soon the bottles were popping and glasses chinking. I think a number of us managed only one drink and some polite conversation before realising that if we didn't get to sleep soon we'd simply keel over.

It was at this point that we had to say "au revoir" to some of the team. We had known there wouldn't be room for everyone to sleep in the guard boats, so a number of rowers headed off to the luxury of a pre-booked hotel room. A number of others decided to fly back to Guernsey.

The next day, with just Colin, Haddi, Karl and me on board, we re-fuelled Tristan and headed down river, in company with the other guard boats, to start our journey home.

The journey back to Guernsey took only two days. Once we were back at sea we could open Tristan's throttles which made a change from tootling along at five knots. The sea was very calm, with a long low Atlantic swell which Tristan took in her stride. Jon and I had a hysterical half an hour trying to teach Haddi how to drink tea with the boat gliding at speed up, over and down the swells. Haddi, polo shirt covered in tea remarked: 'I reckon I've made close on a thousand cups of tea this trip, without spilling a drop – now look at the state of me.'

All the while Colin sat at the navigator's seat smiling and munching his way through a huge box of dried mango and nuts. 'That was fantastic,' he said. 'But never again. You have my permission to shoot me if I ever mention another row.'

Postscript: A few years on....

So far, I have been fortunate with the course of the disease. I am lucky not to have lost mobility or my sight or to be suffering pain. I am fortunate also to have been able to retire early, but most of all I am blessed that our family is still together. For many, life with MS is a daily struggle, full of pain, frustration, heartache and regret. Some families break up, as they cannot cope with the constant demands the disease places on them.

Some 100,000 people in the UK suffer from Multiple Sclerosis. MS is seldom a disease of death; it is however, always a disease for life.

The constant need for welfare and care of sufferers diverts money that might otherwise be used for research. I really wish the £130,000 we raised during the row could have been spent on research, to beat this thing forever, but nursing care must come first.

Our MS nurse is now bringing relief and hope, not just to Islanders on Guernsey who have MS but also to their families and friends. We now also benefit from the services of an MS Physiotherapist and in 2008 we have gained a visiting Neurologist.

The success of the MS nurse has led to the Guernsey Health Services agreeing to fund this post once the money raised by the rowers has been exhausted.

We are all very proud that Colin Fallaize's remarkable services to the MS Society and his huge influence in sport on the Island have been recognised. He received his MBE from Her Majesty Queen Elizabeth at a ceremony in Buckingham Palace.

In typical Colin style, when he heard he had been awarded the MBE he said: 'Doesn't seem right somehow: some people get a disease and I end up with a medal.'

I took over from Colin as Chairman of the local branch of the MS Society and, during my three years as chairman, derived great satisfaction from trying to improve life for all those affected by the disease. We even managed to gain another world record for the Island but this time, although logistically quite demanding, a world record human and teddy bear chain wasn't quite as physically or mentally challenging!

Colin took a well-deserved break from the committee but agreed to be a joint patron. He didn't give up the idea of another row though, only a few weeks after the London to Paris row he said: 'Guernsey to Guinness sounds good doesn't it?' 'Oh no Colin!' I said. 'If you think the English Channel was bad, wait till you experience the Irish Sea; and anyway I thought you wanted me to shoot you if you ever mentioned another row!'

A few more years on – Tragedy strikes and we face a different degree of uncertainty

By the end of 2009 I had still been prevaricating about publishing this book. That year had been a challenge. Both my daughters were, by then, medical students. Katie was at Brighton University and Sophie, our younger daughter, had just completed her first year at Edinburgh University.

Before Christmas 2008 Katie was complaining of pins and needles and the odd neurological symptom that she speculated might be early signs of MS. Katie had recently had a lecture on MS and we all suspected she was falling foul of med student syndrome, where they start to believe they might have every disease they learn about. Also, the chances of MS occurring in three out of four generations are very slight indeed.

In February, Ros and I finally had the chance to catch up with old friends of ours who we first met while sailing 17 years ago in Turkey and have, for the past 10 years been sailing around the world. You might recall from an earlier chapter that we had waived them goodbye as we left

Mallorca. Malc and Lindy Robertson came back to the UK most winters and while we often caught up with them during these visits, we hadn't yet managed to actually join them on their round the world trip. Ros and I at last to caught up with them in Thailand and had the most relaxing and funny two weeks pottering around the islands near Phi Phi.

Malc and I spent a lot of time talking about all things nautical and bouncing ideas and questions off each other about family and business. We enjoyed a level of mutual respect and confidence with each other and I was always delighted that Malc often asked for my views on his business plans. In addition to this, Malc always encouraged me in whatever my latest project was.

Two weeks after we returned from our trip we received the unbelievable news that Malcolm had been brutally killed by pirates. Mercifully, Lindy had escaped with her life but she had suffered the most appalling ordeal and had been tied up and held hostage for 10 hours. Ros and I were beside ourselves with shock and grief and both Katie and Sophie who loved Malc and Lynn as if they were family, struggled in the ensuing months to cope with the anxiety caused by this dreadful act.

Lindy asked me to write and deliver the eulogy at the funeral. While this was all going on, Katie's symptoms had developed further and the night before Malcolm's funeral I went with her to see a neurologist in Brighton. The neurologist stated that he was 95% certain that Katie did have MS. I couldn't believe it. Katie was amazingly stoic about receiving the news, stating that: 'I knew it was MS, I've been convinced for ages.' She was tearful but immediately said: 'I'm not going to let this rule my life.' The next few hours were desperately difficult as Ros heard the news and re-lived the nightmare of receiving such a diagnosis.

The next day, we said goodbye to Malcolm. We decided not to say anything about Katie's diagnosis but, as I sat down after delivering the eulogy for Malc, I sobbed uncontrollably, with the congregation of 400 looking on. I don't know whether I was crying more because of Katie's diagnosis or for the loss of Malc, or just at the sheer injustice of it all.

I placed a small silver Guernsey coin on Malc's coffin. The coin had a picture of a sailing boat with spinnaker flying. I explained to the congregation the significance of Guernsey being Malc and Lindy's first landfall in their round the world trip and went on to explain that In ancient times, boat builders often put a coin under the mast step, to pay the mythical ferry man to convey the souls of dead sailors to the afterlife. Hundreds of people filed past Malc's coffin, to pay their last respects, each placed a flower and now many also added their coins to mine. As the bearers finally moved the coffin out of the Church, the coffin was by now completely covered in flowers and overflowing with coins.

Since that day, Katie has been coming to terms with her MS. She is now benefiting from monthly infusions of the best drug available and she has been relapse free for nearly two years. She completed her junior doctor years and is now a completing her three-year training to become a G.P.

Katie has relapsing remitting MS and, while there is about a 65% of her developing secondary progressive MS at a later date, we are obviously hopeful that advances in therapy will stop this happening.

I couldn't have imagined, all those years ago that the MS Nurse we all worked so hard to obtain for our Island would now be treating my own daughter. I cannot begin to express the comfort Nurse Debbie has bought, not only to Katie but also to Ros, Sophie and me. At the time she was diagnosed, Katie became the 121st person with MS on

Nurse Debbie's database[11]. Now, a few years on, that figure has grown to over 150, making the incidence in Guernsey amongst the highest in the World.

It seems that the uncertainty of life in the Platts household has not, and never will, leave us.

In November 2013, our family suddenly had to face an even more chilling challenge. Ros discovered that she had breast cancer. This news rocked us and tested us nearly to breaking point. But we are not broken. We are having to learn to cope with another and even more serious threat, but our family is still determined to make the best of whatever we have and whatever life can offer.

---

[11] Probably through improved diagnostics, in 2013 Nurse Debbie had 150 islanders with MS on her database.

Appendices

London to Paris Row log - (Row target 83.5 hours*)

Time BST	Latitude	Longitude	Leg NM	Cum Dist	Cum dist. Planned over ground	+/- Schedule nm	
Start 3rd June							
13:04	51 30.103N	000 07.212W					Westminster Bridge
14:00	51 30.280N	000 01.868W	4.50	4.50	4.98	-0.48	
15:00	51 29.755N	000 03.745'E	5.31	9.81	10.37	-0.56	
16:00	51 28.393N	000 14.259E	7.16	16.97	16.97	0.00	
17:00	51 28.160N	000 27.274E	9.63	26.60	24.16	2.44	
18:00	51 29.601N	000 39.802E	10.27	36.87	32.27	4.60	Start of Estuary
19:00	51 28.239N	000 50.832E	6.99	43.86	39.27	4.59	
20:00	51 28.209N	001.00.275E	5.75	49.60	44.29	5.31	
21:00	51 28 680N	001 07.856E	4.90	54.50	49.31	5.19	
22:00	51 28.720N	001 14.475E	4.12	58.62	53.41	5.21	
23:00	51 27.946N	001 20.512E	3.84	62.46	60.01	2.45	
00:00	51 26.527N	001 24.972E	3.11	65.57	63.61	1.96	
01:00:00 Fri	51 24.065N	001 28.597E	3.36	68.93	68.71	0.22	
02:00	51 20.951N	001 28.091E	3.13	72.06	73.31	-1.25	South of North Foreland
03:00	51 17.737N	001 27.335E	3.24	75.30	76.41	-1.11	
04:00	51 14.348N	001 26.792E	3.41	78.71	80.11	-1.40	
05:00			7.03	85.74	82.21	3.53	

Time BST	Latitude	Longitude	Leg NM	Cum Dist	Cum dist. Planned over ground	+/- Schedule nm	
06:00:00 Fri	51 04 742N	001 20.136E	4.18	89.92	91.31	-1.39	Dover Straits
07:00	51 00.203N	001 13.013E	6.36	96.28	97.71	-1.43	
08:00	50 55.236N	001 04.421E	7.37	103.65	104.31	-0.66	North East of CS3 buoy
09:00	50 50.861N	000 56.119E	6.81	110.46	109.41	1.05	
10:00	50 47.995N	000 49.115E	5.28	115.74	114.43	1.31	
11:00	50 45.637N	000 44.262E	3.91	119.65	118.53	1.12	
12:00	50 43.724N	000 39.856E	3.34	122.99	122.43	0.56	North of CS2 buoy
13:00	50 41.453N	000 34.146E	4.27	127.26	126.53	0.73	Shipping Lanes
14:00	50 37.526N	000 33.143E	4.57	131.83	121.28	10.55	Permission granted
15:00	50 32 714N	000 33.112E	4.81	136.65	126.38	10.27	to cross shipping lanes early
16:00	50 28.707N	000 27.289E	5.46	142.10	132.98	9.12	
17:00	50 23.907N	000 24 055E	5.56	147.56	139.58	7.98	
18:00	50 19.158N	000 22.324E	6.98	154.54	145.68	8.86	
19:00	50 14.686N	000 18.153E	5.22	159.76	150.78	8.98	
20:00	50 10.209N	000 15.327E	4.83	164.58	155.88	8.70	
21:00	50 06.798N	000 13.633E	3.58	168.16	160.98	7.18	
22:00	50 05.112N	000 14.122E	1.71	169.87	166.08	3.79	
23:00	50 04 010N	000 14.471E	1.13	171.00	171.18	-0.18	
00:00	50 03.408N	000 13.809E	0.74	171.74	176.28	-4.55	
01:00 Sat	50 00.270N	000 11.103E	3.58	175.32	181.38	-6.07	
02:00	49 55.989N	000 07.522E	4.87	180.18	186.48	-6.30	

Time BST	Latitude	Longitude	Leg NM	Cum Dist	Cum dist. Planned over ground	+/- Schedule nm	
03:00:00 Sat	49 51.928N	000 04.065E	4.63	184.82	191.58	-6.77	
04:00	49 46.583N	000 02.267E	5.47	190.28	196.68	-6.40	
05:00	49 40.998N	000 01.457E	5.62	195.90	201.78	-5.88	Off Le Havre
06:00	49 35.042N	000 01.110E	5.95	201.85	207.12	-5.27	
07:00	49 29.380N	000 01.924E	5.74	207.58	211.72	-4.14	
08:00	49 26.210N	000 05.420E	3.88	211.46	216.77	-5.31	
09:00	49 25.911N	000 13.349E	5.16	216.62	221.87	-5.26	Honfleur Radar Twr to Stbd

River Seine

Actual Time BST	Kilometre Mark	Leg Distance nm	Cum Distance nm	Cum dist. Planned	+/- Schedule nm	
0930	351	2.40	219.02	224.15	-5.13	(Lower limit daylight navigation (348k)
1034	334	9.20	228.22	231.00	-2.79	
1052	328	3.20	231.42			
1101	325	1.62	233.03	235.00	-1.97	
1121	320	2.70	235.73			
1130	316	2.16	237.89	238.29	-0.40	
1214	308	4.32	242.21			
1226	304	2.16	244.37	245.30	-0.93	
1235	301	1.62	245.99			

Actual Time BST	Kilometre Mark	Leg Distance nm	Cum Distance nm	Cum dist. Planned	+/- Schedule nm	
1249	297	2.16	248.15			
1311	292	2.70	250.85			
1325	289	1.62	252.47	253.00	-0.53	
1335	284	2.70	255.17			
1425	276	4.32	259.49	259.00	0.49	
1440	273	1.62	261.11			
1506	267	3.24	264.35	263.00	1.35	Rouen
1600	252	8.10	272.45			
1653	247	2.70	275.15			
1730	241	3.24	278.39	280.00	-1.61	(Limit daylight nav. 225)
1755	236	2.70	281.09			
1900	227	4.86	285.95			
1930	223	2.16	288.11	294.00	-5.89	
2000	219	2.16	290.27			
2100	211	4.32	294.59	300.00	-5.41	section 6.73 knots)
2204	202	4.86	299.45	304.50	-5.05	Amfreville Lock
0316 Sun	161	22.14	321.59	326.00	-4.41	Notre Dame Lock
0419	152	4.86	326.45	329.00	-2.55	
0800	121	16.74	343.19	342.00	1.19	Mericourt Lock

Actual Time BST	Kilometre Mark			Leg Distance nm	Cum Distance nm	Cum dist. Planned	+/- Schedule nm	
0915 Sun	107			7.56	350.75	347.00	3.75	
1000	99			4.32	355.07	349.00	6.07	
1200	82			9.18	364.24	355.00	9.24	
1224	78			2.16	366.40	358.00	8.40	
1300	73			2.70	369.10	361.00	8.10	Andresey Lock
1531	49			12.96	382.06	370.00	12.06	Bourgival Lock
1850**	17			17.28	399.34	382.00	17.34	Suresnes Lock
2013	5			6.48	405.82	390.00	15.82	Finish

(Original figure revised (new figure 9.35 nm less) to take account of route change across shipping lanes midday Friday)

** estimated time

Average speed Thames estuary 7.37 kts

Average speed during sea section 4.61 kts

Avergae speed during Seine section 5.24 kts

Avergae speed in tidal section of Seine 6.73 kts

Avergae speed in non tidal section of Seine 4.83 kts

Avergae overall speed 5.1 kts

* Original target prior to shortening of route resulting from permission to cross rather than go around shipping lanes

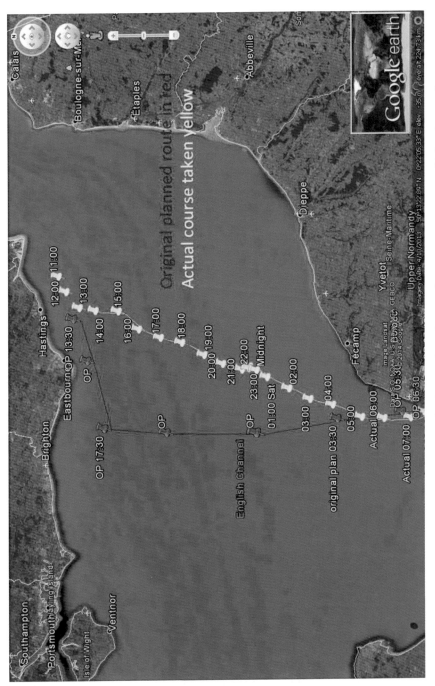

Graphical illustration of planned and actual routes across English Channel

Graphical illustration of planned and actual approaches to River Seine

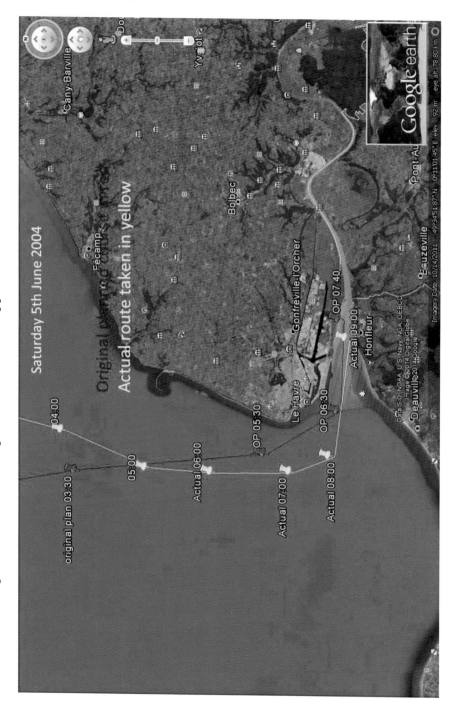

Saturday 5th June 2004